YALE UNIVERSITY
MRS. HEPSA ELY SILLIMAN
MEMORIAL LECTURES

The Origins
of Knowledge
and Imagination

JACOB BRONOWSKI

NEW HAVEN AND LONDON
YALE UNIVERSITY PRESS

Designed by Sally Sullivan Harris
and set in Times Roman type.
Printed in the United States of America by
Vail-Ballou Press, Inc., Binghamton, N.Y.

Published in Great Britain, Europe, Africa, and
Asia (except Japan) by Yale University Press,
Ltd., London. Distributed in Australia and
New Zealand by Book & Film Services,
Artarmon, N.S.W., Australia; and in Japan by
Harper & Row, Publishers, Tokyo Office.

Library of Congress Cataloging in Publication Data

Bronowski, Jacob, 1908–
    The origins of knowledge and imagination.

    (Mrs. Hepsa Ely Silliman memorial lectures)
    Includes index.
    1. Knowledge, Theory of—Addresses, essays,
lectures.   2. Imagination—Addresses, essays,
lectures.   3. Languages—Philosophy—Addresses,
essays, lectures.   4. Science—Philosophy—
Addresses, essays, lectures.   I. Title.   II. Series:
Hepsa Ely Silliman memorial lectures, Yale
University.
BD181.B76   121   77-13209
ISBN 0-300-02192-5 (clothbound)
ISBN 0-300-02409-6 (paperbound)

Grateful acknowledgment is made to M. B. Yeats,
Miss Anne Yeats, and the Macmillan Co. of London
and Basingstoke and to the Macmillan Publishing
Co., Inc., New York, for permission to reprint
"For Anne Gregory," by W. B. Yeats, from *The
Collected Poems,* copyright 1933 by Macmillan
Publishing Co., Inc., renewed 1961 by Bertha
Georgie Yeats.

THE SILLIMAN FOUNDATION LECTURES

On the foundation established in memory of Mrs. Hepsa Ely Silliman, the President and Fellows of Yale University present an annual course of lectures designed to illustrate the presence and providence of God as manifested in the natural and moral world. It was the belief of the testator that any orderly presentation of the facts of nature or history contributed to this end more effectively than dogmatic or polemical theology, which should therefore be excluded from the scope of the lectures. The subjects are selected rather from the domains of natural science and history, giving special prominence to astronomy, chemistry, geology, and anatomy. The present work constitutes the forty-fourth volume published on this foundation.

CONTENTS

FOREWORD

A physiologist friend of mine once recounted how, as a refugee from Germany studying in a British country school during World War II, he was cruelly teased for his bookishness and Jewishness by the schoolmates, until a sudden change took place. One evening the students were taken to a neighboring town for a public lecture on science in the modern world, and from then on the students treated their refugee colleague with a new respect. The lecturer who in one hour had made both culture and Jewishness respectable and even glamorous to his youthful audience was Jacob Bronowski.

I choose this anecdote because it illustrates one aspect of Bronowski's protean personality, his role as educator, a role that throughout his life he performed not so much in the classroom as in a variety of other situations: in his stimulating conversation, fed by an immense store of knowledge; in his scholarly lectures in which he always strove, as he put it, to reveal "the hidden likeness in diversity"; and finally in his approach to the mass audience in the monumental achievement of "The Ascent of Man."

Two of Bronowski's earlier books, *Science and Human Values* (1956) and *The Identity of Man* (1965), are particularly relevant to the present context. Both were, like the book presented here, the texts of series of public lectures delivered in academic settings. Both represented audacious leaps from the domain of science into explorations of central aspects of the human condition: What message does science have for human conduct? How does human experience become transformed and integrated into the personality of the individual, into what Bronowski called a human "self"?

In those books Bronowski outlined an approach to scientific psychology based on an analysis of the structure of the two creative activities, science and art. The interpretation of these two activities within the intellectual enterprise and the impossibility of any artificial separation of them from one another are themes that consistently recur in Bronowski's teaching.

The roots of these themes are made more explicit in the Silliman Lectures. Knowledge and imagination, according to the author, are two inseparable aspects of the intellectual experience. The imaginative moment is as creatively central to science as to poetry or to figurative art. The mind acts upon the natural world in the creation of knowledge in the same way as it acts on the elements of human sensibility in bringing forth a poem or a painting or a symphony.

Bronowski's wish to define and clarify the role of imagination as the unifying element in the variety of intellectual activities—in fact, as the creative element in human psychology—was indirectly responsible for the fact that the

Silliman Lectures appear only now in the form of a transcript of the lectures as delivered at Yale in 1967. It had been his hope to have these lectures appear as one of a pair of books, the subject of the other being the nature of the artistic enterprise. This plan did not materialize. The stupendous effort of preparing the series of television programs for "The Ascent of Man" demanded all his energies. And death made nought of further plans.

The structure of *The Origins of Knowledge and Imagination* is different from that of other books by Bronowski. The lectures are both more technical and more openly didactic. A deceptive beginning, introducing the theme of appearance versus essence by way of a charming poem by Yeats, promptly leads into a discussion of some of the most complex areas of knowledge, where the scholar— the "natural philosopher," as Bronowski chooses to call himself—comes to grips with the epistemological questions that concern the nature of limits to human understanding. It is a tribute to Bronowski's brilliancy as a scholar and an interpreter that he can make his discussion of such questions understandable and often fascinating.

The nature and power of human language as a creative instrument for ordering and giving structure to human experience; the nature of time and the meaning of relativity; the limits of physical measurements as interpreted by quantum mechanics; the boundaries to formalization of knowledge inherent in the axiomatic structure of mathematics— these and other topics become accessible, indeed humanized, by the author's insistence that they should be looked at not just as constructions within science but as expressions of the human mind defining itself in action.

Throughout the book the interest of the reader is stimulated by the interplay of two themes that recur almost like melodies in a sonata and give the text its intellectual unity. These themes are the role of conscious human activity in the creation of knowledge and the imaginative content of that knowledge.

It will not surprise the readers of these lectures to learn (should they be unaware of it) that besides his many accomplishments as mathematician, philosopher, linguist, and educator, Bronowski was also a prominent Blake scholar, the author of the seminal book *William Blake and the Age of Revolution* (1965). Blake, artisan, painter, print-maker, poet, and political visionary, had in his own time something to say that was not so different from what Bronowski wants us to learn from his lectures: that the integrity of the doer should be matched by the vision of the thinker; that such vision consists as much as of what the viewer projects outward as of what it receives; that passivity before the supposedly inexorable march of events —whether the Industrial Revolution or the mechanization of society—can only lead to slavery; and that freedom must be created by the interaction between human wisdom and the physical world.

Like his great contemporary Goya, Blake was an artist who viewed the human condition with strength, compassion, and imagination. Both artists pictured human folly as the stuff of nightmares, to be dissipated by the light of reason. Bronowski has confidence in human reason. His lectures breathe optimism, an optimism not unlike that of the thinkers of the Enlightenment, but sobered and refined by the modern view of nature and of the place of the human mind within it. Whether or not one shares Bronowski's optimism, one must be grateful to him for proposing it. Once again, as in that provincial English town where he lectured one evening thirty-five years ago, Bronowski brings to his audience a message of human harmony.

S. E. Luria

Cambridge, Mass.
1977

1
The Mind
as an Instrument
for Understanding

I will start by reading a poem by W. B. Yeats called "For Anne Gregory." It is a conversation between a man who asks her questions and herself. The first verse is by the interrogator who says to her,

> "Never shall a young man,
> Thrown into despair
> By those great honey-coloured
> Ramparts at your ear,
> Love you for yourself alone
> And not your yellow hair."

To this Anne Gregory replies,

> "But I can get a hair-dye
> And set such colour there,
> Brown, or black, or carrot,
> That young men in despair
> May love me for myself alone
> And not my yellow hair."

And the interrogator then has the last verse and the last word; he says in answer,

> "I heard an old religious man
> But yesternight declare
> That he had found a text to prove
> That only God, my dear,
> Could love you for yourself alone
> And not your yellow hair."

I choose to introduce this lecture and the series with that poem because it states a perennial theme in Yeats and the underlying theme of these lectures: how we get experience which is not directly physical through physical means. For "yellow hair," you will have to read "human vision," "speech," or any of the other fundamental human abilities which are mediated by the physical senses or by physical capacities, and which nevertheless we believe give us knowledge of the outside world.

Since the word "knowledge" occurs in my general title, "The Origins of Knowledge and Imagination," I ought to begin by saying that I am going to be talking about epistemology, although I prefer to use an eighteenth-century, indeed, a medieval phrase, "natural philosophy." By natural philosophy I mean that enterprise of the human mind which attempts to trace lawfulness in nature, dead and living, but which is not directed to specific inquiries into how this or that law works. Philosophy in the sense in which I practice it, natural philosophy, is concerned with lawfulness rather than with laws and with the general nature of laws rather than with the specific structure of this or that law. Natural philosophy was one of the three topics (moral philosophy and metaphysical philosophy were the others) to which one graduated in medieval universities after having studied the seven liberal arts. I shall be talking about natural philosophy most of the time, though the last of my lectures is obviously concerned also with moral philosophy.

I believe that we need to review the whole of our natural philosophy in the light of scientific knowledge that has arisen in the last fifty years. It really is pointless to go on talking about what the world is like (as much of philosophy does) when the modes of perception of the world which are accessible to us have so changed in character. And we become more and more aware that what we think about the world is not what the world is but what the human animal sees of the world. My program in these lectures, therefore, is the program which Immanuel Kant proposed back in the 1760s, when he was still a practicing scientist and had only just begun to venture into philosophy. He wrote a number of books and papers whose basic message was this: our knowledge of the outside world depends on our modes of perception, and I am going to write philosophy as a description of the structure of the world as seen by man.[1]

Unfortunately, a great revolution took place in Kant's life in or about the year 1768, when he read a paper by Euler which was intended to show that space was indeed absolute as Newton had suggested and not relative as Leibnitz suggested.[2] (You must remember that the eighteenth century was still full of this enormous sense of world division between Newton and Leibnitz. It was impossible to discuss philosophic doctrines without including them, just as impossible as it is at this moment to talk about Marxism in the same terms in Moscow and in London. So in the eighteenth century the question of whether Newton's view of the world or Leibnitz's view of the world was right profoundly affected all philosophy.) After reading Euler's argument about the nature of space in 1768 Immanuel Kant published a book which for the first time proposed

1. See F. S. C. Northrop, "Natural Science and the Critical Philosophy of Kant," in *The Heritage of Kant,* ed. G. T. Whitney and D. F. Bowers.

2. L. Euler, "Reflexions sur l'espace et le temps," *Memoires de l'Academie Royale des Sciences et Belles Lettres* 4 (Berlin, 1748): 324–33.

that there must indeed be such a thing as space, that events must fit into it, and that we must be conscious of it a priori.[3] And since Kant died in 1804, long before new ideas about space—I was going to say, had been thought of, but that is not true, they had been thought of—but long before they had been published, we have all been hagridden with this idea that the world is there and that our modes of perception do not much influence how we interpret it; that we can get at the nature of the world without much bothering about the apparatus that we use.

I think that is wrong. And since one of the things that happened in your lifetime and mine has been the substitution of what you might call a Leibnitz universe, the universe of relativity, for Newton's universe, it seems to me very appropriate that we should think that out again. Just as, in the poem, you cannot love the girl without being conscious of the fact that she has yellow hair, you cannot see the world without the intervention of the physical senses.

So much for the word "knowledge" in my title. I should also explain to you that I have used the words "the origins of knowledge" rather than the "grounds" of knowledge or the "nature" of knowledge because I want in particular to take us through the biology of the modes of perception, of speech, and of symbolization and therefore, of the evolutionary steps by which man has reached his biological situation.

3. I. Kant, "Concerning the Ultimate Foundations of the Differentiation of Regions in Space" (1768), in *Kant: Selected Precritical Writings and Correspondence with Beck,* translated with introduction by G. B. Kerford and D. E. Walford (New York: Barnes & Nobles, 1968).

As soon as we talk about the perception of the outside world, we are in fact doing philosophy as if we were an engine and as if the modes of perception of the engine were essential to our interpretation. Now, I do not think that it is disgraceful to talk of human beings as biological engines, provided that we are very clear both about what "biological" means and about what "engine" means. And that is why in my fourth lecture I shall be talking about what engines can and cannot do, in particular what computing engines can and cannot do; and why in this lecture and in the next I shall be talking about what animals can and cannot do. So you might say that these are lectures about how the world looks, seems, and behaves to human beings, thinking of the human being as a special kind of animal and of the animal as a special kind of engine.

Running all through these lectures and underlying my interest in these problems is a quite simple question: What kind of an animal is a man? I am going to propose one clue to the answer in a moment or two, but I want to introduce it by saying something about the relation of the view of man as an animal and the view of man as a spirit.

All animals are very special. They are certainly not simple engines. And man is a very special kind of animal. At the moment, there is a fashion in talking about man and animals that I suppose was begun by Konrad Lorenz and that has been made popular in this country recently by Robert Ardrey,[4] which seems to me to be, if I may say so, oddly childish. It takes us right back to all the quar-

4. Robert Ardrey, *The Territorial Imperative: A Personal Inquiry into the Animal Origins of Property and Nations* (London: Collins, 1967).

rels about evolution in which Darwin and Huxley and Bishop Wilberforce were engaged just over a hundred years ago. Let us take Lorenz's last book, *On Aggression*.[5] Well, the book is really quite simple—indeed, since you could write it all on a small postcard, I naturally was impatient at going through it at great length. What it has to say is that you only have to look at mammals in general in order to see that most of them require some built-in aggressive behavior in order to maintain themselves. Therefore, the conclusion is that human beings, who are obviously mammals, display aggressive behavior and therefore it is very important in their lives; it is very important for us not to forget it; wars are expressions of this kind of behavior—you can fill in the rest for yourselves.

Now I do not at all deny that rats are rather aggressive animals. But it seems to me strange to say that this proves something about human beings, when the obvious thing is that rats are all down in the skirtingboard somewhere whereas we are all sitting up here. If everything that we have to know about ourselves is stuff that we can get from the rats, why aren't the rats in here and why aren't we scurrying in the wainscoting?

People have been very impressed by the fact that many animals, not only mammals but birds and fish as well, display territorial behavior. That is, there is a piece of territory which they regard as their own and from which they chase others of their kind. And so, everybody says territorial behavior is important to human beings and Robert Ardrey has written a book about it. Now the point about

5. (London: Methuen, 1963).

territorial behavior is very clear. It is that the robin red-breast sings in a loud clear voice in order to keep other robin red-breasts away from the bit of territory that he is on. But except for singing in the morning in the shower, I have never known a human being to utter sounds for this purpose.

I give you these examples only in order to make the very clear-cut point that, while we shall be talking in these lectures about human beings as a special kind of animal, what we are interested in is the word "special." Of course it is terribly important that we should share a lot of features with other animals. But it is of critical importance to ask ourselves what features which other animals do not possess have given human beings the very special capacities with which we are concerned in these lectures: the ability to utter cognitive sentences (which no other animal can do) and the ability therefore to exercise knowledge and imagination. There are extremely rudimentary societies, like that of Tierra del Fuego when Darwin visited there, where there is virtually no science, even in the sense of magic and prediction, and virtually no art. But "virtually no" and "no" are as different as cheese and chalk. So let me say at once that to me the most interesting thing about man is that he is an animal who practices art and science and, in every known society, practices both together.

That is not the only thing that differentiates man from the other animals, of course. Man alone adopts the frontal attitude in sexual intercourse; only women in any of the primates have breasts permanently; we are almost the only primates that do not have a bone in the penis. We

could go on in a hundred and one details, all of which
are extraordinarily interesting, all of which no doubt have
their place in human evolution, both in what they have
done and in why they have come about. Although we
could spend the rest of the day talking about such facts,
I will have to leave you to read up on them for yourselves.

The word "imagination" is also in my title. I want you
to think of the following words: visual, vision, and visionary; and image, imagery, imagination. My reason for
choosing these words is of course that I want to come to
the word "imagination." But I want you to see what always strikes one with surprise in looking at this kind of
word. Almost all the words that we use about experiences
of the kind that go into visions or images are words connected with the eye and with the sense of sight. "Imagination" is a word which derives from the making of images
in the mind, from what Wordsworth called "the inward
eye." But the very fact that Wordsworth could use such a
phrase makes it very clear how much the intellectual activities of man are eye-conditioned.

If you think of it, there are essentially only two groups
of arts that human beings practice. One group includes
arts which are mediated by the sense of sight, like sculp-
ture and painting; the other group includes arts which are
mediated by speech and sound, like the poem and the
novel and the drama and music. Of the human senses
these two dominate our outlook. The sense of sight dominates our outlook on the outside world, whereas the sense
of hearing is used by us largely in order to make contact
with other people or with other living things. There is a
very clear distinction in the way in which most of the

time we use vision to give us information about the world and sound to give us information about other people in the world.

I should just say in passing that, of course, other senses enter the picture. For example, it is said that Eskimos make those very small sculptures because they carry them and feel them. And one of the senses which is not even one of the five classical senses, the kinesthetic sense, is obviously part of our appreciation of dancing or moving. But by and large, this division between the arts of sight and the arts of sound (including music) is clear cut.

The world of science, however, is wholly dominated by the sense of sight. If you were to say to yourself, suppose that Newton had been born blind and that all science since then had been carried out by blind men, would our knowledge of the world be anything like it is today? The answer is patently no.

The place of the sense of sight in human evolution is cardinal. Human beings have evolved, we now believe with confidence, along a line which goes back from us to the most primitive and unspecialized of the primates. Among the living primates, our closest relatives are the great apes, then, more distantly related, the old world monkeys, then tarsiers, then lemurs, and finally the tree shrews, animals which may not be true primates at all, but which share the way of life of our earliest ancestors at the beginning of the primate line. The evolutionary gap from that tree-shrewish ancestor to ourselves is of the order of seventy-five million years.

Now these are all animals that have lived in trees, in-

deed, the tree shrew looks very much like the squirrels
that run around on the lawns here at Yale. And the interesting thing about them is that they require those special
senses that animals need in order to live in trees. And
the sense of sight plays a radical part in the whole of this
evolutionary scheme. An animal was not a success in the
trees if it did not have good eyesight. It is extraordinary
to look at modern representatives of all these species and
observe how large an area of their brains is occupied by
the visual cortex, how dependent they are on the sense of
sight. However, if we take the living primates as clues to
our common ancestors, we can trace the evolutionary
development of vision. For instance, the apes and the old
world monkeys have color vision; some new world monkeys may not. The nearer we come to man, the more animals depend on stereoscopic vision, that is, their two eyes
are fixed in such a way that the fields of vision overlap.
This is only possible by rotating the face so that the eyes
come forward. To be sure, some long-snouted animals, like
lemurs and dog-faced baboons, manage to have stereoscopic vision by looking out over the tops of their muzzles.
But taking primates as a whole we can see how the face
has developed from the funny little squirrel-like tree shrew
(and its fossil ancestors), whose eyes stare out on either
side of its sharp nose, to the flattened visage of ape or
human.

But if you compare a human being with even the most
sharp-eyed of the great apes, say with a chimpanzee,
our vision is incredibly more delicate. These are all animals that see very well, their visual fields tend to overlap,
they tend to have stereoscopic vision, as you go up the

scale they tend to see in color, but their ability to discriminate fine detail (which can be tested in a very simple way) is not comparable with that of human beings. You will see now why I attach so much importance to the sense of vision, because we have become almost wholly dependent on it, and its emergence as the major mode of perception of the outside world has undoubtedly been *the* great culturally formative ability for human beings.

Now how does the sense of vision work? Well, it is really not very long ago that people used to think that the eye worked like a television camera: it scanned the scene, it produced a lot of dots, it shot them to the back of the head and then the brain got to work and saw what went on. The sense of vision is not remotely like that, however, and the human brain does not work like that at all. And we cannot really do better than to say at this stage how it works in order to show you how complex a mechanism the human brain is and what strange problems it has had to solve.

I have already said that even the great apes are not able to exercise fine discrimination in the way that we are. And, therefore, you would suppose that, if you are going to have an animal like man which is bent hell for leather on getting fine discrimination, the optical apparatus of the eye must be improved, a better lens must be developed, the retina must be divided more finely, and so on. Nothing of the kind. The most interesting thing about the whole physiological development of the human eye and brain is that fine discrimination is not achieved in that way.

I shall come to this point again and again, particularly

when I talk about brains and machines in the fourth lecture. The brain does *not* achieve fine discrimination by pushing fine discrimination forward in the senses and by producing a more sensitive physical apparatus. If I may anthropomorphize the brain for a moment, the brain has had to solve the problem of achieving fine discrimination with a coarse apparatus. And in many ways you can say about all human problems, whether in science or in literature, whether physical or psychological, that they always center around the same problem: How do you refine the detail with an apparatus which remains at bottom grainy and coarse?

Well, George Wald has just won the Nobel Prize for step number one in this. He showed that when a single quantum of light strikes a rod or a cone in the eye it untwists the visual purple that has been wound up by the body and makes it fall back to the lower energy state of, roughly speaking, the Vitamin A molecule. (That is not precisely true, but it is sufficiently true to give you a clear picture of what happens.) The eye is full of rods and cones, and in each of them there is a fluid called visual purple which is bleached when light strikes it. Once it has been bleached a rod or cone cannot see again until it has been revivified. The step from purple to colorless (like all steps from any color to no color) represents a lowering of energy; a single photon of light untwists the molecule of visual purple and lets it fall back into the state which approximates that of normal Vitamin A. It is a beautiful piece of work. I am happy to say that when I introduced George Wald two years ago when he gave the Man and Nature Lectures in New York, I said that everybody ought to know about this piece of work because it was in the Nobel Prize class. And I am glad that people in Scandinavia were listening.

Now this short description tells you enough to make it clear that the eye does not form a continuous picture. Because if it is full of rods and cones and if single photons of light activate them, then the thing must be jumping about like mad with spots of light here and there. Moreover, it does no good for a photon to hit a rod or cone that has just been struck—they must be rewound before they can receive again. So we have a very coarse, grainy surface, which is rather like that of old-fashioned newspaper photographs. In addition, there must also be a substratum of noise because you cannot have an eyeful of over a million of these units without some of them going off wrong, even in total darkness. You must realize that not only does a machine go wrong every so often, but so does any apparatus that man or God can devise. Therefore, there are always quite a number of rods and cones in the eye which are giving up a bleaching signal, an electric signal, saying "we have been struck by a photon," when, as a matter of fact, it is a lie, they have not been struck. So one of the problems is to get rid of this noise.

In that respect the eye is a delicate instrument. The noise level at any given instance is only of the order of five photons, and ten photons is more than enough to tell you that a real signal exists. That is really a very delicate response. In fact the eye overcomes these difficulties by sending back into the brain signals which contain all kinds of safety devices.

Think of the sharp outline of this piece of paper that

I am holding, and ask yourself if it is going to appear sharp on an eye which is being triggered off by the rain of photons I described. The answer is: of course not. There must be an extremely wavy edge of shadow against light in my eye which somehow goes to the brain as a straight edge. There must be many errors according to what photon comes through at this moment, what part of the eye has already been struck, and so on. The very grainy nature of both energy and matter makes this certain. Now there is nothing at the back of the head which acts like a kind of screen on which this information falls. And yet somewhere in the brain there arrives at this moment a hail of electrical blips which says "that's a straight edge." And the reason it does this is because the eye is so wired up among the rods and cones that it actually looks for straight edges.

The very odd thing about the eye of the frog, the cat, the rabbit (the ones which have been studied most carefully) is that the signaling of boundaries to the brain is the main thing that they are wired up to do. And indeed in the frog's eye it looks as if there is actually a mechanism which signals whether the boundary that is now crossing the eye is straight or curved (which is important for frogs).

This is a very strange form of machinery. It does not send back simple signals; the back of the retina has an elaborate wiring circuit which picks out conjunctions which are meaningful in the outside world. Boundaries are such conjunctions. So are differences in color. The eye never sends back a spot saying "that seat is red." It essentially sends back this kind of information as I move the eye across: "All the red spots surrounded by green boundaries are not being activated but the green spots surrounded by red boundaries are being activated—and that means red."

This is the way in which precise information from coarse units is reached by elaborate wiring systems among the units. There are two very interesting things to be said about this. (Let me say that this is largely the work which Hartline pioneered and for which he, Granit, and Wald won the Nobel Prize.) [6] One is that we know from experiments with kittens (who also have stereoscopic vision) that you are born with some of the connections which are wired in the eye. But it is also clear that, even though a kitten is born, for instance, with a mechanism which makes it focus both eyes at the same time, unless the kitten practices this mechanism from the moment it opens its eyes, the mechanism will not work. So you have a very extraordinary biological phenomenon: even prewired circuits in our sense organs have to be kept alive and tuned by use, at least by use in early childhood. This is, no doubt, one of the ground reasons why deprivation of any kind in early childhood is so catastrophic both in animals and in human beings.

The other thing that I want to make clear is this. It may seem very smart that the eye is ready-wired to see straight boundaries or curved boundaries, contrasts of light, and so on. But you must also realize that every machine of this sort always pays a price for the things it can do very

6. Ragnar Granit, H. K. Hartline, and George Wald shared the Nobel Prize for Physiology in 1967 for their discoveries concerning the primary physiological visual processes in the eye.

cleverly—namely, by not being able to do other things. And one of the things that the eye is not able to do is to look at nature with a fresh, open vision as if it were not looking for straight edges and contrasts of color. Exactly because search mechanisms for these things are built into the eye, we are constantly deceived about the nature of the outside world because we interpret it in terms of the built-in search mechanism.

I made this excursion into the mechanism of the eye in order to say how central it has been to the evolution of human beings. We stand at a peak in visual discrimination; we are utterly dependent on it. And I want to end by saying we are dependent on it not only in looking outward but in looking inward.

The abilities that we have in the way of memory and imagination, of symbolism and emblem, are all conditioned by the sense of sight. It is sight which dominates this kind of sequence, how we think of things that appear in the mind. And I come back to saying "visual," "vision," and "visionary"; "image," "imagery," "imagination." Now imagination is a much less mechanical gift than that of the eye as I have described it. But because it is squarely rooted in that, it is an ability which human beings possess and which no other animal shares with them. We cannot separate the special importance of the visual apparatus of man from his unique ability to imagine, to make plans, and to do all the other things which are generally included in the catchall phrase "free will." What we really mean by free will, of course, is the visualizing of alternatives and making a choice between them. In my view, which not everyone shares, the central problem of human consciousness depends on this ability to imagine.

2
The Evolution
and Power of
Symbolic Language

I will recapitulate in the briefest way what I said in my first lecture. I said that my program was the program in natural philosophy which Immanuel Kant had set himself when he left physics to begin to write about philosophy. He abandoned that program in 1768; it seems to me high time to carry it through. The program is to ask what our knowledge of the external world rests on when we think of ourselves not as having God-given insight into it, but as being human animals penetrating it with the physical gifts we possess.

As an example of how we sense the world, and how we communicate that information to the brain, I took the sense of sight. I chose it, first, because it is of dominant importance in all the primates and in man specifically, and, second, because it is a typical but very well worked out example of how the impressions of the outside world reach us. Even when we think about the inside of our consciousness rather than the outside world, we use the metaphors of the eye, of what Wordsworth called "the inward eye." We do that whether we are thinking about strictly scientific descriptions, like "vision" and "image," or highly poetic ones like "visionary" and "imagery."

I demonstrated that the eye works subject to the handicap of all cellular systems; namely, that it has to exercise fine discrimination using very coarse units. That is a wonderful problem. It is really *the* problem of the end of the twentieth century for anyone who seeks to examine all aspects of nature. How are we able to exercise fine discrimination when the units with which we work (like the rods and cones in the eye, like the neurons that lead back to the brain) are so coarse? This kind of discrimination can be achieved because the system of interconnection is such that a great deal of overlap is created, and as a result not only the brain but the eye itself makes inferences about the world. We are not able even to receive visual impressions except by a process of indirect inference. Inferences are, therefore, at the root of all our mental processes, even those exercised directly through the senses. To understand inference in its logical implications is of the greatest importance, and my next lecture in particular will be much concerned with what one might call the logical formalization of inference.

Today, however, I want to talk, as the title says, about "the evolution and power of symbolic language." The word "evolution" will occur again and again in what I have to say. When Kant wrote his program evolution was an idea barely in the head of Charles Darwin's grandfather, Erasmus. Kant died in 1804; Charles Darwin was born in 1809. It is thus natural that nowhere in Kant's idea of how knowledge is based on the human senses is there a conception that the evolution from animal to man might provide a clue. In fact, what I have to say about human evolution really has only been known in the last twenty years.

The fact that natural selection in human societies has been so largely dominated by human cultures themselves for at least the last million years is a fundamentally new idea. I am going to be talking about language and speech, and the most obvious way to begin is to say again "visual," "vision," "visionary." These are three words which visibly have the same root (that was not intended to be a joke; it was merely meant to demonstrate how much such vision words stay in one's mind) and yet in which there has been an enormous shift of context and application. Now everybody knows that human beings can do that, that they can shift the contexts and applications of words, and everybody knows that there is not the slightest evidence that animals can do anything like that. Yet it is unlikely that human speech as we know it is even as old as half a million years. How did we progress so incredibly swiftly from making the kind of noise that a chimpanzee makes to making the kind of noise that a human being makes?

Well, so far as physical equipment is concerned, the transformation is easy to understand. Roughly in the last half million years, beginning at most about a million years ago (which is absolutely no time at all on the evolutionary scale) the brain of human beings and their immediate ancestors enlarged at a prodigious rate. So far as we can tell, the brain of *Australopithecus,* a human precursor who lived roughly a million years ago, weighed about a pound to a pound and a half. He was small by our standards (though not much smaller than I) and therefore his brain to body weight ratio should be interpreted with a certain generosity; let us say that if he were brought up to full size now his brain might be regarded as weighing one and a half to two pounds. The average weight of brain in this audience is three pounds, and there are certainly several people here whose brains weigh more than four pounds. However, brain weight (yesterday I heard it called, enchantingly, "biomass") is really *not* the critical issue.

The crucial change in the human brain in this million years or so has been not so much the increase in size by a factor of three, but the concentration of that increase in three or four main areas. The visual area has increased considerably, and, compared with the chimpanzee, the actual density of human brain cells is at least 50 percent greater. A second increase has taken place in the area of manipulation of the hand, which is natural since we are much more hand-driven animals than monkeys and apes. Another main increase has taken place in the temporal lobe, in which visual memory, integration, and speech all lie fairly close together. And the fourth great increase has taken place in the frontal lobes. Their function is extremely difficult to understand (nothing that I say today will be right in ten years time); but it is clear that they are largely responsible for the ability to initiate a task, to be attentive while it is being done, and to persevere with it.

The speech area just over the temporal lobe does not exist in any other animal. That puts the discussion of speech into a quite peculiar category, because there are no experiments you can do with animals which give you any information about speech. Almost all the information that we have comes from the study of human beings who have suffered brain injury of some sort. And, of course, that kind of work is always extremely suspect because you never see a normal brain. People like Penfield and Roberts in Canada and Luria in Russia have worked with literally hundreds of cases, but they have never had a whole, well-integrated, normal man under the knife.[1]

Study of the speech area, therefore, has to be pursued through methods which fifty years ago would have been

1. W. Penfield and L. Roberts, *Speech and Brain Mechanisms* (Princeton, N.J.: Princeton University Press, 1959); A. R. Luria, *Higher Cortical Functions in Man* (London: Tavistock, 1966).

regarded as highly speculative. But these methods have become very respectable now because they are exactly like the kind of reasoning that is used in astrophysics. And when we talk about the evolution of, say, the speech area, most of our guesswork is of the same kind as the conjectures about whether or not the universe originated fifteen billion years ago with a big bang. In almost all right-handed people the speech area lies on the left. That is true for certainly over 95 percent of right-handed people. It is also true for the great majority of left-handed people. Such human anatomical peculiarities suggest that language and speech as human beings possess it is in some way different from animal communication.

Now I would like to forget about anatomy and function and settle down to the question of how this has come about. There are two schools of thought. There are those who think that obviously evolution has been continuous and therefore the speech area and the gift of speech must be continuous with animal sounds. Then there are others, like Noam Chomsky and in particular Eric Lenneberg, who think that human speech is an altogether specific gift discontinuous from any animal function.[2] I do not think that they are right. I think that their view is a misinterpretation which largely rests on a misunderstanding of the way evolution has worked in man. It misses, in my opinion, the fact that human evolution has, I repeat the phrase, been dominated so completely by human culture itself. For the past million years, human culture has been the most important selective influence in making men what

2. Noam Chomsky, *Cartesian Linguistics* (New York: Harper & Row, 1966); Eric H. Lenneberg, *Biological Foundations of Language* (New York: Wiley, 1967).

they are. So I think that human speech is indeed a continuation of animal communication, and the interesting thing therefore is to see where it differs.

It would be delightful to spend a long time on the enchanting subject of animal communication. The displays of the bower bird when courting his mate, the dance of the honeybees when directing foragers to sources of nectar, the way in which the great crested grebe picks up bits of weed from the bottom of a lake and presents it to his spouse while preening his feathers and flapping his wings —these are subjects to which I cannot do justice.

The central thing to keep in mind about animal communication is that it is communication: an animal makes a noise or emits some other signal which influences other animals, not itself. It would be pointless to say it is trying to influence other animals. I do not even know what you are trying to do when you communicate, and I certainly do not know what animals are trying to do. But it is clear that, for instance, an animal utters a cry of alarm because natural selection has operated in favor of those animals which uttered the cry of alarm and in favor of those other members of their species which heeded the cry and took cover. It is an obviously well worked out self-correcting survival mechanism. And it does not operate only within a particular species, because Thorpe has observed birds heed the alarm cry of a bird of an entirely different species whose cry has no sound in common with their own alarm cry.[3]

It is clear that this kind of noise—cries of alarm or

3. W. H. Thorpe, *Bird-song: The Biology of Vocal Communication and Expression in Birds* (Cambridge: Cambridge University Press, 1961).

hunger, courtship gestures or noises, cries to signal that the individual has found food—form a very restricted vocabulary, which, so far as we know, is built into the animal genetically, both in emission and in response. Sometimes the messages are quite complicated. For instance, according to von Frisch, honeybees signal the location of a rich source of nectar by running a sort of figure eight in which the direction of the main line points to where the food is, and the speed at which the figure is run is an estimate of the distance away.[4] And this system seems to work very well. Von Frisch's most recent work has shown the story to be rather more complicated than this,[5] but in effect it is still only a mechanical system. Although only dwarf bees actually run on the flat outside the hive, more sophisticated bees run vertically on the combs. Such bees substitute the direction of gravity for the direction of the sun and they measure this angle by the sun as against the vertical. And when they do not see the sun, because they are sensitive to polarized light, they know where the sun is anyway. Even so, we are in the presence of the transmission of a direct signal, and a direct, entirely mechanized response.

Even quite sophisticated animals like the baboon or the rhesus monkey have a total vocabulary of at most a hundred signals, probably nearer forty. About half of these are sounds, and the other half are gestures. And that is

4. Karl von Frisch, *Bees: Their Vision, Chemical Senses and Language* (Ithaca, N.Y.: Cornell University Press, 1950).
5. Karl von Frisch, *Tanzspreche und Orienterung der Bienen* (Berlin: Springer-Verlag, 1965); translated by L. E. Chadwick (Cambridge, Mass.: Harvard University Press, 1967).

a vocabulary that every member of the tribe knows, and every member interprets the signals in exactly the same way.

The baboons, for instance, send watchers to the outskirts of their colonies because they lead rather complex lives. (Like human beings, they have come down off the trees, and they are not really very suited to running about on land, and so they keep very careful guard.) And when you hear a baboon make that barking sound which says, "Danger," all the baboons scatter. I have seen a film in which this sound has been reproduced on tape, and the baboons go on scattering without ever any thought. They usually do not say "Oh, Jim's barking again, he's always crying wolf. Pay no attention." It usually wouldn't be wise to wait and see if a leopard really did appear in order to check up on Jim. However, if the animal giving the alarm is a young one, the troop adults may well check out the source of alarm before running away on the word of an inexperienced youngster. You know, fifty years from now we shall all realize that primates have many rudimentary human attributes. But today we are making simple black and white distinctions, and it is essential to understand that we are in the presence not of a language but of a code of signals. The primates' code is like the things that the military use which is simply set out in a book, and one five-digit number represents one thing, and another five-digit number represents another thing, and you cannot move them around. Zhinkin in Russia has made a most elaborate attempt to decode the language of the baboon in order to show that a baboon might possibly say the same thing in two different ways.[6] And he has written a very weighty paper, full of mathematics, at the end of which the analysis shows that although baboons can say a great many things in a very small number of grunts and cries, they have only one way to say any one thing.

Now human language differs from this in a number of respects. Perhaps I can introduce the first difference by saying something about the most interesting of all animal signals, silence. You will remember a passage from "Silver Blaze," a Sherlock Holmes story, in which the conversation goes like this: Inspector Gregory says to Holmes, "Is there any other point to which you would wish to draw my attention?" And Holmes says, "To the curious incident of the dog in the night-time." Gregory, who is an absolute sucker for falling into this kind of trap, replies at once, "The dog did nothing in the night-time." "That was the curious incident," remarks Holmes.

Now we know as the result of work which Fabre first published in 1853 that in fact doing nothing is quite an important animal activity.[7] When he was observing grasshoppers, Fabre was much struck by the fact that, when he stayed still, they were all dashing about like mad, yet they never seemed to take fright. But whenever *he* moved, all the grasshoppers in the field started furiously moving

6. N. I. Zhinkin, "An Application of the Theory of Algorithms to the Study of Animal Speech: Methods of Verbal Communication between Monkeys," in *Acoustic Behavior of Animals,* ed. R.-G. Busnel (Amsterdam: Elsevier, 1963), pp. 132–80.

7. Jean Henri Casimir Fabre, *The Life of the Grasshopper,* trans. A. Teixeira de Mattos (London: Hodder & Staughton, 1918).

about and taking fright. It took him a long time to realize that the reason was this: when a grasshopper is about to jump, he makes a little noise, which for convenience I will call "goodbye." Then all the other grasshoppers know that he is about to move. If the grasshopper moves without first announcing that he is going to move, that is the curious incident of the dog in the night-time—and the other grasshoppers know that something is wrong. And you can see for yourself that this has an enormous selective advantage because the poor animal that is killed without being able to utter that farewell "goodbye" is in fact alerting all his neighbors to the fact that there is something wrong. Similar signals have been found for rooks and other birds. Now there again you have this mechanical thing, silence as a one-way signal that spells "Danger." Silence is one of the most interesting of human reactions, and of course among human beings it does not necessarily signify danger. So let us now look at the way in which human language differs.

First of all, the human response to another human signal is rather slow, compared to most animal responses. Unlike the bees that run off to fetch nectar, we do not answer at once. Indeed, we have a rather long delay period. This is certainly something physiological that happened quite early in human evolution, this delay time in the circuit between input through the ear and output through the mouth. It really is the first thing that makes human response possible.

We sometimes teach ourselves how to make this kind of delay. My father used to say to me, "When you are really very angry, count up to twenty before you say anything at all." And someone to whom I told this recently said that in his household, which was a Roman Catholic one, you were asked to say a paternoster first—a rather more pious version of the same insistence that there shall be a delay after the input in order to avoid uttering a hasty reply. Why? Because you are angry. And that shows you what the delay has done to human speech in general. We are able to separate information from emotional content, or *affect,* when we interpret or frame messages.

Now that is an enormous evolutionary step. We have no evidence of that in any other animal (except perhaps my friend the chimpanzee whom symbolically you must always think of as grinning over my shoulder and saying, "Well, it is not quite as simple as that"). We are able to get at what the message says and to separate it from the emotional charge which the message also carries. That is not true of animals. For them the message is a unitary signal. And for reasons of natural selection you can see that this has got to be so. This conclusion is fairly recent, however. For instance, when the dancing of the bees was first discovered, people said, "Oh, the bees are just excited." People knew that the bees danced before they went to a rich source of nectar, but they supposed that this was just the result of general excitement. Bees do dance when they are excited but they also dance when they are not excited. And they are just as accurate in describing their figure eight, in pointing it the right way, and in controlling the speed of the dance which carries the message whether the source of nectar they have discovered is rich or poor. They do not dance so many times when they have discovered a poor source of honey: but whereas in a state of excitement we would go wrong, you and I, pointing the wrong way, going too fast, and so on, they do not.

This extraordinary way in which the code message does not lose its accuracy as the result of its emotional charge is of the first importance. But it is, of course, also an enormous handicap to animals because it really means that they cannot convey information at all. They can really only convey instruction. Information, like the cry of "wolf," allows you to interpret it. If you cannot separate emotional charge from the information, then you cannot interpret it. This is why I constantly make a distinction between information and instruction, and say that all animal and machine languages are essentially instructions. The subject of my lectures, "the origins of knowledge and imagination," would be inconceivable in a world of animal or machine languages because you cannot convey *knowledge* in a language in which these two things are always and indissolubly linked in the message. For the same reason you cannot say that one animal has a good style and the other animal has a bad style, because we put style into what we say by deciding what kind of color or emotional affect to give the statement.

Now this first step in the evolution of human languages is undoubtedly a straightforward physiological one. But the steps from here on are largely dominated by a step that went hand in hand with it, and that is the emergence of foresight in human beings (I mean to say, hominids and prehominids) somewhere between a million and two million years ago.

We have clear evidence that at least half a million years ago (perhaps, as recent discoveries suggest, as much as two million years ago or more [8]) there were primitive early types of man who not only used stone tools, but actually stored them in advance. And this curious find at Olduvai of pebbles, some of them unworked pebbles, which have been brought a couple of miles from the river bed and kept ready for use in the dwellings is the first and spectacular sign of one of those great developments that is unique to the human race, the ability consistently to foresee a use for things in advance.

Human beings are not the only tool users. Indeed, you have all seen enough photographs by Jane Goodall and her husband to know that chimpanzees use long sticks or stems to poke into ants' nests. They even prepare the sticks by pulling the leaves off stems, and they go some distance to gather them, but they never lay in a supply in advance. When they see the ants' nest they start looking round and say, "It would be a good idea to have a stick." Similarly, members of one species of Darwin's finches in the Galapagos Islands (which, because they behave like woodpeckers but have only the beaks of finches, require some probe to get at their food) tear off thorns and poke under the bark with them, which is an extraordinary ability. But none of them spends the evening going round and tearing off a nice tidy supply of a dozen probes for tomorrow. Foresight is so obviously of great evolutionary advantage that one would say, "Why haven't all animals used it and come up with it?" But the fact is that obviously it is a very strange accident. And I guess as human be-

8. See L. S. B. Leakey, ed., *Olduvai Gorge*, vol. 1 (Cambridge: Cambridge University Press, 1965).

ings we must all pray that it will not strike any other species.

Foresight is tied with the later development of the brain in the second thing that is special to human speech. This is what I call the "prolongation of reference," the ability to use language so that it applies not only to what is going on now but to what went on or to what will go on. Animal signals naturally do not have this reference. Prolongation of reference is a part of human speech which is connected with the high selective advantage that foresight conferred.

If you will allow me an aside, there is nothing Lamarckian about this conception of cultural selection that I am putting forward; it is quite simple. As soon as foresight occurs, as soon as there are men and women in the species who know how to pick up a stone in advance, then there is an obvious advantage in favor of those who are good at handling stones and in favor of those who have foresight. In no time at all they either get all the girls or all the men; they have many more offspring; and they can keep themselves alive when other people starve. It is the ordinary selective mechanism operating. So although the use of the tools is a *cultural* phenomenon, that cultural phenomenon imposes itself and causes natural selection in its own favor. And one of its reflections in language is the prolongation of reference into the past and into the future.

The third feature that is unique to human speech is *internalization*. I said earlier that animals address their species at large, or possibly even members of another species, either to frighten them off or to communicate with them, but they do not, so far as we can tell, address themselves. The internalization of language is a human phenomenon of profound importance.

I believe that it goes hand in hand with these questions about tool use and tool making for the following reasons. Visualize a man who is chipping a stone tool of the kind that we have now found to be at least a million years old. To him every stroke is an experiment, and he can judge its success by looking at the stone. He throws away ones that go wrong (most of those we find, of course, are ones that were thrown away). He also sometimes has models, and the model is not only a record, but a blueprint. A very important aspect of every technological tool is that it is not only a record of how it was made, but a blueprint of how others are to be made. It carries its own prolongation, its own history, and its own look into the future. And in order for the man who is making a tool to ask himself whether he is successful or not he must internalize, he must carry on an interior dialogue with himself of the kind that all of you have carried on when you whittle something or when you have stood over the stove and something has gone wrong.

Human beings have a wholly unique gift in the use of language, and that is that they talk to themselves. Everybody does it, all the time. At this moment every one of you is carrying on an internal dialogue and a considerable part of it is actually taking place in words. You have a lot of irrelevant thoughts about what you are going to wear tonight or where you are going to be or how long the lecture is going to last, but you do not put such thoughts into words because they are not specific, you are just conscious that you are thinking about how much longer without actually saying it to yourself. But as soon as you say to yourself, "I wonder whether the chimpanzee is really exceptional or whether the orangutan is the same," then at once you are thinking something highly specific, and such things cannot be thought without words.

And that leads me to point number four, which is that gift linguists usually call the productivity or generativity of language. Because of this strange gift one can say "John loves Lucy" and "Lucy loves John" and, at least in a language like English which does not have any exterior signs of cases, they are indistinguishable except that the words are in a different order and the phrases mean different things. Now we know no animal language in which you can rearrange the noises and get a new meaning. (I should warn you there is a small amount of dispute about this. There are bird lovers who say that birds do rearrange their songs and that they do mean something different, and there are even some insect lovers who say the same thing about insect noises.) But by and large and keeping to the simple outline, this structure in human language is unique.

This grammatical structure is called *stratification,* making layers of language, and it depends essentially on the fact that this message can be broken down into three different concepts, a man called "John," a girl called "Lucy," and an action called "love." No animal does this. Indeed its universe is not of that kind. That is why it is so important to seize this concept. The animal lives in a universe in which the animal and universe are in constant communication, and the animal does not separate any action from the outside universe. You can see for yourself how this would happen. If, like a dog, for instance, you lived wholly by smell, you would find it very difficult to visualize what was going on. Human beings analyze the outside world in a different way. They analyze it into objects and actions. How? It begins in language itself.

You know there is a splendid biblical phrase, "In the beginning was the word." Now although this is a very important thing to say about human beings, it is quite untrue about the evolution of messages in general. In the beginning was the sentence. An animal utters a cry which is a sentence, and he cannot take it apart and put the back first and the front afterward. Indeed, when you try to do this to birds, for instance, when you try to play their song to them after rephrasing it and arranging the figures differently, they are as distressed as a musician who hears the wrong movement played first. It does not go that way. The animal message is a sentence, and when we started speaking, like the baboons, we must have started in sentences. And the great thing that happened to us was that we learned to take the sentence apart. Nobody knows how this happened, and it is really the great mystery about how human language came to be. Nobody would believe that it could happen, except for the fact that it actually has.

Let me give you an illustration. The chipmunk has three different alarm signals. One of them says that there is danger from a bird, one of them says that there is danger from a snake, and one of them says that there is danger from a largish ground animal. It makes these without error however excited it is; indeed, the greater the danger, the more accurate the signal is. Nothing in the chipmunk's vocabulary enables it to separate the idea of danger and the personality of the predator. What has happened in human language is that from the multiplicity of signals saying danger from here, danger from there, we have slowly been able to generalize the conception of danger and particularize the conception of the predator. And in that way, by what I call *reconstitution,* we have built a world of outside objects, a world which does not exist for animals.

Now, both linguists and philosophers (Wittgenstein in his later work, for instance) are full of the miracle that we can arrange words in different ways. But all of them overlook the central problem and point of interest, which is that before you can arrange words in different ways something else must happen. You have got to ask yourself, "How did the words come to fall out of the sentence in the first place?" And that is a real miracle, the one depicted in the Byzantine mosaics in which the Virgin Mary conceives the Christ when a ray of light falling from the star enters her ear and the inscription says, "In the beginning was the word and the word was made flesh," at least, it is the modern interpretation of that miracle.

Now our consciousness depends wholly on our seeing the outside world in such categories. And the problems of consciousness arise from putting *reconstitution* beside *internalization,* from our also being able to see ourselves as if we were objects in the outside world. That is in the very nature of language; it is impossible to have a symbolic system without it.

I shall be speaking in the third and particularly the fourth lecture of all the difficulties that arise from this remarkable and wholly human gift that allows us first of all to separate ourselves from the outside world. We see that there is a world of things; we recognize it as permanent; we move it about; we are able to rearrange it in our heads from "John loves Lucy" to "Lucy loves John," which no one supposes to be the same statement. And with that goes inevitably a sense of ourselves, sometimes also as an outside person. The Cartesian dualism between mind and body arises directly from this, and so do all the famous paradoxes, both in mathematics and in linguistics, to which I shall return.

3
Knowledge
as Algorithm
and as Metaphor

L et me recall that the program that I have set myself in these six lectures is that which Immanuel Kant proposed early in his life, to construct a natural philosophy which was based on the physical ability of human beings to receive and translate their experience of the outside world. This was an enterprise which Kant abandoned when he actually came to write philosophy on a large scale.

In my first lecture I showed that even the perception of the senses is governed by mechanisms which make our knowledge of the outside world highly inferential. We do not receive impressions which are elemental. Our sense impressions are themselves constructed by the nervous system in such a way that they automatically carry with them an interpretation of what they see or hear or feel. I said in my first lecture that, in common with the other primates, but to an even greater extent, we get most of our knowledge of the external world through the eye. I also said that the sense of hearing is equally important to us because that is how we get most of our information about other people.

Therefore, I devoted my second lecture to sketching what seems to me a sensible evolutionary sequence for speech, for symbolic language. I pointed out that only human beings are able to make, to internalize, and to exchange with one another utterances which have a purely cognitive content. We pass knowledge to one another, that is, information which does not have the preprogrammed force of an instruction. Animal signals, by and large, are pure instructions.

I suggested that this cognitive content has evolved in

human language by a process which is continuous from animal signals. The animal sentence has been progressively broken down so that the sentences that we exchange contain words: words which either stand for objects in the outside world or for actions. This analysis of the outside world is bound up with human language. It is closely related to the visual imagination in human beings, and by its means we dominate and conjure the external world.

I was brought up as a very orthodox Jew, and I was therefore not permitted to utter the name of Jehovah, and that is absolutely of a piece with all those savage communities in which you must not utter certain names because they give you power. The idea that one can conjure the world with names, with nouns, and even with verbs is a familiar belief among primitive peoples.

Consciousness, then, is our mode of analysis of the outside world into objects and actions. And I pointed out at the close of my second lecture that it at once posed a problem; namely, that we also think of ourselves as objects and we therefore also apply language to ourselves. We treat ourselves both as objects of language and as speakers of language, both as objects of the symbolism and as symbols in it. And all the difficult paradoxes which go right back to Greek times and reappear in modern mathematics depend essentially on this. I shall be concerned in my next lecture with the implication of these paradoxes for the use of symbolism, both in literature and in science.

Let me write for you two symbolic expressions. The

first is one which occurs in the work of Newton; it says that "the gravitational attraction between two massive bodies is proportional to the product of their masses divided by the square of the distance between some point in each mass." If any single utterance by a scientist has reshaped history, it is this, the law of inverse squares. Ludwig Boltzmann's gravestone was inscribed with the symbol for entropy, $S = k\log W$, and I suppose if Newton had had any control over what was to be put on his gravestone, he would have chosen $G = k\dfrac{mm'}{r^2}$. Now we all understand that as a symbolic expression which describes in some way the structure of our experience.

Let me now write for you another symbolic expression which I take from "The Auguries of Innocence" by William Blake. I take a couplet almost at random; this one says,

> A Robin Red breast in a Cage
> Puts all Heaven in a Rage.

Now the extraordinary thing about that verse is that it appears to have none of the formal structure of Newton's formula. Yet it is a highly general statement and everybody in this room knows exactly what it means, and I mean *exactly*. My "exactly" may not be your "exactly," but in some way we all know with an immediacy which we derive from language and experience what

> A Robin Red breast in a Cage
> Puts all Heaven in a Rage.

means. I would say that everybody understands this, whereas there must be a good many people in the audience who, in fact, are taking $G = k \dfrac{mm'}{r^2}$ on trust.

Well now, I wish I could lecture on generalizations of the form of "a Robin Red breast in a Cage," but I can only do so much on one occasion. There are two things, however, I want to say about both of those statements. One is that they are both general statements; let no one tell you that this quotation is only a particular statement. It derives its general appeal to us all from its high specificity, and that is the miracle of this kind of remark; but it is a statement which says something about the human situation and not just about *a* robin or *a* cage. Secondly, neither statement has the form of a syllogism; neither says all As are Bs or any of those things that occur in the textbooks on logic in which sentences are always written as if they described classes. It is my view that that is very foreign to human language, that no scientific statement and no poetic statement is of the form, "all As are Bs." This is what these two have in common. This kind of symbolism is a highly active kind. Do not be deceived by the equals sign. It says something which describes what happens when you do something.

In discussing statements of this sort, scientific statements, I am going to treat science as a language. I am going to say that this formula is a sentence in the language, that all such statements are sentences in the language, and that the way we construct this language mirrors the way human language evolved. However, I should make one preliminary about it and explain to you that science is a rather peculiar language because it only contains statements that are, in the context of a particular theory, true. We do not, for instance, say, "Well, $G = k\dfrac{mm'}{r^2}$ is a sentence in this language. And another sentence in this language is $G = k\dfrac{mm'}{r^3}$." In the language that we are discussing, $G = k\dfrac{mm'}{r^3}$ is not a sentence.

There are statements in the language of science which have a simple and fairly descriptive form. For instance, when Kepler said in 1609 that the planets run on ellipses round the sun as focus and sweep out equal areas in equal time, that is a fairly descriptive sentence. The sentence which Newton wrote about the gravitational attraction is a more abstract sentence and in fact summarizes the description of what Kepler said. For the purpose of the discussion today that is not an important difference, and I will not labor it.

We are always looking for a language in science which mimics or mirrors the structure of reality. And the problem is, How does it do that? My claim is that it does it in exactly the same way in which human language evolved from animal language, by analyzing the sentence into constituents which represent separable entities in the outside world—things or actions. So science constantly seeks in the descriptive sentences for separable entities which can either be perceived in the outside world or, more often, have to be inferred speculatively in the outside world.

The structure of reality is not self-evident, and the structure of the scientific language is not self-evident.

When Wittgenstein wrote the *Tractatus* during the First World War, he thought that you could make a language out of ordinary discourse, more or less, which could somehow give you the structure of reality. He said that the very fact that "I love you" and "I hate you" have the same kind of structure tells you something about the relations, that the relations are built into the grammar. Now, it is true that the relations are built into the grammar, but we have to get a very specialized grammar, the grammar of science, as Karl Pearson rightly called it, in order to demonstrate the structure.

During the Second World War Craik tried to show that the nervous system actually mimics these structures within our brain, and that was an equally unsuccessful attempt.[1] No, we have to tease out the structure from the observational sentences when we make them into abstract sentences. How do we do that? Well, we do it essentially by treating nature as, in Leibnitz's phrase, a gigantic cryptogram, a gigantic series of coded messages. And we seek to decode it in such a way that entities emerge which are conserved under various changes and transformations.

Mass is such an entity. Newton was not able to define mass; nobody in a sense can define mass. Indeed, you could say that the great step from Newton to Einstein was that Einstein was the first person who gave a reason for what had already puzzled Newton, namely, why gravitational mass and inertial mass are the same mass. Of course, you and I think we know what a mass is; we know it in the sense that we know what we think we are

1. K. J. W. Craik, *The Nature of Explanation* (Cambridge: Cambridge University Press, 1943).

saying when we ask for a pound of butter. But that is a knowledge which itself comes late in the development of language. Incidentally, it also comes late in the development of children. Remember that children before the age of four are always very puzzled when you pour liquid out of a tall beaker into a broad beaker and say to them, "Is it the same amount of liquid? Which would you rather have?" Without exception, children say they would rather have the orange juice in the tall narrow beaker. And if you say to them, "Why?" they say, "Well, there is more." And then if you say, "But there is not more; I can pour it into here and I can pour it back," they are not in the least persuaded. Why should they be? Why should they regard it as a law of nature that orange juice remains invariant in mass when you pour it from a narrow thin beaker into a small flat beaker? That is a real theorem.

And I mention that theorem only to remind you that all our prejudices about the external world tend to be built into the language of science. Then, when somebody shows that the whole thing was nonsense, that we put our prejudices into it, we are always taken aback. I mean, in 1900 if you had said to somebody, "Could my watch run faster if I were standing at the equator than at the north pole?" everybody would have said, "But that is rubbish! Only children think that kind of thing." When in 1905 Einstein wrote a paper in which he said just that, everybody said, "But that is marvelous. What a child's vision he has." Which is true.

Let me give you one more example. What about *r,* the distance between these two masses? Well, I suppose in theory you could say that you could take a foot rule, lay it down something of the order of 10^9 times, and say, "We have proved it, that is the distance between the earth and the moon." But, of course, you cannot do astronomy with that kind of distance. And it is very interesting to see how these concepts again have to be teased out of the cryptogram of nature.

Let me tell you one of the most beautiful and simplest experiments on this that was ever conceived. It was conceived by a man called Olbers; it is called Olbers's paradox and is more than a hundred years old.[2] Olbers said, "The sky is full of stars, and they are obviously pumping energy into space. Now we can assume that the universe is reasonably old, and that therefore it has settled down to some kind of state of equilibrium. If that is so, then every object in the universe has reached a stage at which the amount of energy that is being radiated to it from the star must be exactly the same amount which it is radiating back." And so Olbers said, "It is very clear that if we go out into the night sky, it should be as bright as daylight because there is all the energy in a state of equilibrium, and there should be no local disturbances. How can we avoid this?" And, indeed, there was no way of avoiding it at the time. The only possible way of avoiding it that could be suggested was that the universe was rather young and was only just settling down, which seemed slightly improbable.

How do we avoid this? Why do we now say that it is really quite understandable? We can say this because

2. Wilhelm Olbers, "Uber die Durchsichtigkeit des Weltraums," *Bodes Astronomisches Jahrbuch* (1826), pp. 110–21.

Bondi made the following beautiful argument: "The stars are pumping energy into space, and it ought all to be coming back. It ought all now to be well mixed up, like the hot and the cold water in the bath. If it is not coming back, where is it going? It must be going into a volume of space which is greater than that from which it originated." And so Bondi says, "We can do a very simple experiment. We can say that there are three possible states for the universe: it might be contracting, it might be of stationary size, or it might be expanding. If it is contracting, then night ought to be brighter than day because there ought to be more energy coming in simply from the background than the sun is actually supplying. If it is stationary, then night and day ought to be equally bright. And if the universe is expanding, then night ought to be dark." I invite you to perform that experiment tonight. Go out and look, and when you observe that it is dark, you will have made the fundamental observation which shows that the universe is expanding.

We had that information a hundred years ago at least, but until people did terribly expensive experiments with analysis of red shifts and so on, nobody was willing to believe this explanation. But let me invite your attention to the word "expanding." What does it mean? It means that our measure of distance in this universe between us and any other galaxy must be growing larger. Do we have any way of actually measuring this? Of course we do not. We can only do it because the whole language in which we are writing "mass" and "radiation" and "distance" defines things like distance in such a way that all these things come out to make a consistent language. The thing about nature is that when you challenge her with questions as we have just done with Olbers's paradox, you rely on the fact that she does not cheat, that she gives back consistent answers.

If we treat our knowledge of the external world in this way, then we are constructing a language of science which has three features. There are, first of all, symbols which stand for concepts or inferred entities which have the character of the words in these sentences. Then there is a grammar which tells us how these things are to be put together, so that for instance $G = k\dfrac{mm'}{r^2}$ is a grammatical sentence. If you did not put r^2 down but r^3, that would be ungrammatical and the sentence would not be allowed in the language. And finally there is a dictionary of translation which relates a sentence like this to specific problems like determining the period of the moon.

After all, when Newton thought of that, the first thing he did was to calculate the period of the moon. And then he said modestly, when he told this story to his housekeeper, "I found it to answer pretty nearly." He made the period of the moon twenty-eight days so he felt that r^2 was right. These are the three characters of the language of science. The grammar is essentially the rules of operation specified by the axioms; the dictionary of translation is essentially the way we apply the sentences to our common experience; and the symbols or concepts are the solutions of the cryptogram.

Let me give you a different kind of sentence.

$$2NaCl + H_2SO_4 = Na_2SO_4 + 2HCl$$

In the seventeenth century Mr. Glauber made Glauber's salts. And after about another hundred years we learned to write his reaction in the form that if you mix salt with sulphuric acid you get Glauber's salts and hydrochloric acid. Now if you actually were to read Glauber's description, which is full of words like "muriatic acid" and other splendid phrases that I am afraid I have forgotten, you would not, of course, recognize it as the same reaction. Why not? Because you have all been brought up with a code in which NaCl is what you say for salt and H_2SO_4 is what you say for sulphuric acid. But, of course, the whole thing has been translated into a kind of Morse code. And what has been elucidated by the Morse code is that this sodium atom here is an element and that this hydrochloric acid is not an element—a fact which was much in dispute in the time, say, of Humphrey Davy. So that the code teases out the elementary symbols. We solve the cryptogram by doing this. And I do not have to tell you that if you were now to write this in terms of its valences and in terms of the free electrons and so on, you would be breaking down the code step by step into the codes that we now have for nuclear processes. This is why I say that we are making the language. We are making the symbols by the challenge of question and answer, which gives us real statements about the world that we then break down.

I want to come back to this because it reminds you that the grammar has to do with explanation, the dictionary has to do with description, and the symbols have to do with those concepts with which the whole of our consciousness is now full but for which the only evidence for most of us is that somebody told us in a lecture or that it says so in the textbook. Words like hydrogen and helium, nuclear processes, inhibition in biology, inhibition in psychology have become new words in our vocabulary. But they owe their existence to being decoded out of statements of this kind.

I have been giving you a highly personal account of how we practice science. And the obvious question is "Are we inventing the whole thing?" You may say to me, "Aren't you just a thoroughgoing idealist? Do you really think that there *are not* any atoms?" I spoke of Boltzmann and the inscription on his gravestone a little while ago. Ludwig Boltzmann committed suicide in a fit of depression. Why? Because he could not persuade his colleagues that atoms were real. It may not seem to you something to take your life over, but it was to him. The irony, of course, was that had he only held his hand for another year or two, all his colleagues would have been persuaded.

Now, are the atoms real or are they not? And if the atoms are real, are the electrons real or are they not? When we do this decoding, are we discovering something which is in nature, or are we not? Are we creating the concepts out of which we make science, or are they there hidden all the time? Now this is a tremendous intellectual bifurcation. And also a fairly emotional one. For example, the world is pretty well divided into people who are proud of being machines and people who are outraged at the thought of being machines. And the world is, therefore, pretty well divided into people who would like to think that our analysis of nature is a personal and highly imaginative creation and those who would like to think that we are simply discovering what is there.

I wrote the chapter on twentieth-century science for the UNESCO history.[3] If you read it, you will find that it carries behind it a streamer as long as a comet's tail of violent phrases of dissent by young Russian scientists saying: "This is all a terribly idealistic picture. This man does not believe that atoms are real," and so on and so on. Now these questions are not idle ones. Picture yourself for the moment in 1867, a hundred years ago. Supposing you had then asked yourself, "Well, is it real? Is Newton's gravitation a real thing?" Everybody would have said, "Well, of course." Shortly after Newton published the *Principia* in 1687–88 Richard Bentley, the great classical scholar of Trinity College, asked his permission to give some sermons on Divine Providence.[4] And the force of these sermons was that we now understood what Divine Providence was because it was really gravitation. I am simplifying Bentley's sermons somewhat, of course. But the point is that Bentley was enormously impressed with the fact that we now understood in some way how God worked, how nature worked. And from the time of Newton until well into the last century everybody was persuaded that this was so.

3. J. Bronowski, "The New Scientific Thought and Its Impact," in *History of Mankind: Cultural and Scientific Development,* vol. 1, pt. 1, edited under the auspices of UNESCO by K. M. Panikkar and J. M. Romkin (London: Allen & Unwin, 1966), pp. 121–65.

4. Richard Bentley, *Sermons Preached at Boyle's . . .* (1692) (London: Frances Macpherson, 1838).

Everybody was persuaded that we understood the great truths of science, had understood them since the time of Newton, and that what we were now doing was filling in the details. At the end of the last century there were physicists who were perfectly willing to say that there was no need to produce another Newton because there was nothing as fundamental as gravitation for another Newton to discover. And after all, they had the excellent evidence of Adams's and Leverrier's discovery of a planet that no one had observed, one whose existence they had predicted entirely because the perturbations that they observed could only be explained by the presence of another planet, and there it was.

Since then, the world has fallen about our ears. There is almost no scientific theory which was held to be fundamental in 1867 which is thought to be true in that form today. We have lived through a century of the most amazing firework display of new discoveries. Not discoveries of a superficial nature, but ones which have radically altered our whole picture of nature. In 1899 when Max Planck could not make the continuous equations work to match the experiments of his colleagues on black body radiation, he finally made up his mind that radiation came in discontinuous lumps. And that afternoon, when he took his little boy for their usual walk, he said to him, "I have today made a discovery as profound as Newton's." Those were very prophetic words. And the only sad thing about them is to say that the little boy whom he took for a walk was, in fact, murdered by the Nazis because he took part in the plot against Hitler's life in 1944.

From the moment that Max Planck made that statement, we have had a constant upset of the accepted no-
tions. $G = k\dfrac{mm'}{r^2}$ is no longer regarded as a picture of
the ultimate reality in nature. In 1905 Einstein published
the first paper on relativity, which made it clear overnight
that there was something wrong with this concept. And
then in 1915–16 he published the great paper on general
relativity, which substituted an essentially geometrical view
of space-time in its place. If I may translate into geometrical terms, this really said, roughly speaking, that
these two masses attract one another because they form
depressions in space-time; and those depressions tend to
make them run together just as if you put two lead balls
into a bowl of jelly. Well, that is a fundamentally different conception of the world. It is a fundamentally different decoding of virtually the same sentences. No one
would have thrown Newton out of the window if there
had not been sentences which went wrong. If the peri-
helion of Mercury had remained where it was supposed
to be, nobody would have been very troubled.

The new theory, of course, always subsumes more ef-
fects than the old. But the remarkable thing is that when
it is discovered, it also wholly changes our conception of
how the world works. Well then, was the decoding all a
fiction? Is gravitational force a complete fiction? Is Einstein's view of relativity now a fiction since it is by no
means in as good odor as it was in 1915–16? I regard
this as a very important question. I regard it as a particularly important question in an audience like this

which is not wholly composed of professional scientists.

Now I believe that everybody in this room is real. I really believe that you are all there. Moreover, I believe that your blood is circulating just the way that Harvey said, and not the way that Galen said. In other words, I believe that all the kind of scientific descriptions that we can make about one another are perfectly real. And yet, I believe that any theory that we as human beings make at any point in time is full of provisional decodings which to some extent are as fictitious as the notion of force in Newton. How can this be?

In my view, the answer is as follows. I believe that the world is totally connected: that is to say, that there are no events anywhere in the universe which are not tied to every other event in the universe. I regard this to some extent as a metaphysical statement, although you will see, as I develop it in the next lecture, it has a much more down-to-earth content than that. But I will repeat it: I believe that every event in the world is connected to every other event. But you cannot carry on science on the supposition that you are going to be able to connect every event with every other event. Even when you set a computer such a simple problem as playing a good game of chess on the hypothesis that the computer is really going to think out every consequence, it breaks down hopelessly. It is, therefore, an essential part of the methodology of science to divide the world for any experiment into what we regard as relevant and what we regard, for purposes of that experiment, as irrelevant.

We make a cut. We put the experiment, if you like, into a box. Now the moment we do that, we do violence to the connections in the world. We may have the best cause in the world. I may say, "Well, come on, I am not really going to think that the light from Sirius is going to affect the reading of this micrometer!" And I say this although I can see Sirius clear with the naked eye, and I have the impertinence to say that though the light of Sirius affects my rods and cones it is not going to affect the experiment. Therefore we have always, if I may use another Talmudic phrase, to put a fence round the law, to put a fence round the law of nature that we are trying to tease out. And we have to say, "For purposes of this experiment everything outside here is regarded as irrelevant, and everything inside here is regarded as relevant."

Now I get a set of answers which I try to decode in this context. And I am certainly not going to get the world right, because the basic assumption that I have made about dividing the world into the relevant and the irrelevant is in fact a lie. In the nature of things it is bound to give me only an approximation to what goes inside the fence. And whether I treat that as a statistical approximation, or whether I get out some other concept, I am doing so in less than the total context of the world. Therefore, when we practice science (and this is true of all our experience), we are always decoding a part of nature which is not complete. We simply cannot get out of our own finiteness.

Now such decoding can certainly lead to good laws. If what we judge to be irrelevant is not very relevant, they will be good laws. But it does not follow that they give you the conceptual picture of what is in the world at all. And essentially the reason why we have made such enormous changes in our conceptual picture of the world in the last seventy years is because we have had to push out the boundaries of the relevant further and further. Every time we do so, we have to revise the picture totally. Now there is nothing to help us in the decoding. We have to do it in the same way that we invent any word in the human language—by an act of pure imagination.

Let me close by reminding you of what Newton actually did on the day that he conceived $G = k\dfrac{mm'}{r^2}$. He said to himself, "If I throw a ball, it will fall to the ground. If I throw it harder, it will fall a little further off. If I throw it harder still, it will fall still further off. I must be able to throw it just so hard that it falls exactly as fast as the horizon, and then it will go all the way around the world." Beautiful. Full of assumptions about the world being round, and how the ball would behave and so on, but nevertheless a gorgeous, highly imaginative conception— a wonderful piece of visualization. Newton saw it all. He drew a lovely diagram. The ball will fall all the way round the world. How long will it take? It is easy to calculate, roughly ninety minutes.

Well, of course, in 1666 when Newton thought that, nobody was willing to build expensive pieces of apparatus in order to send men round the world to see whether they came back in ninety minutes. That test was reserved for our highly intelligent generation. Newton did not have any subsidies, grants, funds, Secret Service money. But he had the moon. He said, "Of course, I cannot throw a ball round the world, but let me now picture the moon as if it were a ball which has been flung round the world— 250,000 miles up, but still, it is up there. How long will

it take to go round the world?" Well, now it is more difficult. He knew the value of gravity at the earth's surface,
so that was easy to calculate for the ball, but he did not
know the value of the earth's gravity for the moon. He
said, "Let us suppose that it is given by an inverse square
law. Now, how long will it take the moon to go around?"
It comes out at twenty-eight days. As Newton said, "They
agreed pretty nearly."

Now there is the kind of imaginative conception that
we put into the laws of nature. How? When we isolate it
from the rest of the universe and say, "That is the part
of it that is going to count. I am not going to be concerned about the perturbations created by Mars and so
on." And of course, Newton's was a tremendous mind.
You would never get Newton to say, "It came out right."
"They agree pretty nearly," said Newton, not forgetting
about Mars and Venus and everything upsetting it all.

Now we begin to see where the path from metaphor to
algorithm always goes. When Newton saw the moon as a
ball that had been thrown round the earth, he was initiat-
ing a gigantic metaphor. And when it finished up, it was
in a calculable form, it was an algorithm (a formula with
which you can calculate). And that is the path from metaphor to algorithm—from the Blake phrase to the Newton
formula—that every scientific theory has to follow because it is a human section of the totality of experience
which excludes some of the connections which are there.

I will explain next time what importance we ought to
attach to the connections which we break when we impose
a theory, and why this view makes truth by correspondence
(namely, at the dictionary level) and truth by coherence

(namely, at the grammar level) match. It is one of the central problems of philosophical discourse. I also will be talking about how the inside and the outside of the world hang together, but I shall be talking about it in terms of the brain.

I do not want to finish today without reminding you of one last metaphor because I want you to know how our picture of the world is always influenced by the metaphors that we inject into it. Newton had the apple and the moon; but before him, Kepler had had the idea that there was a universal gravitation.

Kepler wrote a book about a journey to the moon in which he said, "Gravity will not stop at the top of the mountains [which is what most of his contemporaries thought], the earth's gravity will go on to the moon." [5] Now that was a wonderful idea for Kepler to have. But then he asked himself, "How would it fall off?" And he had a curious idea. He said, "Well, if it were an open space then, of course, it would fall off like light as the square of the distance. But you see, the earth is in a flat orbit round the sun, so that the sun's force is only being spread over the plane and, therefore," said Kepler, "probably gravity only falls off like this." There he was wrong. But the exciting thing is to understand why he was wrong.

He had got hold of the wrong metaphor. But behind it lay a very curious, much more ancient metaphor. Why did he ever think that masses attracted one another at all?

5. *Somnium, Sive Astronomia Lunaris,* composed c. 1609, published posthumously (Sagan and Frankfurt, 1634). English translation by P. F. Kirkwood in J. Lear, *Kepler's Dream* (Berkeley: University of California Press, 1965).

Well, it is very difficult to trace this. But so far as one can see, Kepler, who had a very mystical turn of mind (the very book that I am quoting from is called *Mysterium Cosmographicum*), was probably influenced by a neo-Platonist called Nicholas of Cusa who thought that all matter in the world attracted.[6] Nicholas of Cusa appears to have taken this neo-Platonic idea from an imposter of the fifth century, a father of the Church who called himself Dionysius the Areopagite. Dionysius the Areopagite (who turned out, as I say, not to be the person he claimed to be) had produced the following argument back in the fifth century. He said, "God's love is universal; it infuses the whole of nature, and it therefore infuses every piece of matter. And, therefore, not only does God's love draw every piece of matter to him, but every piece of matter must be drawn to every other piece."

6. On Kepler's mysticism, see, for example, W. Pauli, "The Influence of Archetypal Ideas on the Scientific Theories of Kepler," in *The Interpretation of Nature and the Psyche,* trans. P. Silz (New York: Pantheon, 1955).

4

The Laws of
Nature and the
Nature of Laws

I n my third lecture I gave an account of science as a language which has been constructed in much the way that I had suggested all human languages have evolved. And I said that on decoding the cryptogram of nature we arrive at a language of true sentences to which three kinds of entities contributed. As a result of decoding, we pick out inferred entities or units or concepts for whose existence we have no direct evidence—gravitation was one example I gave, also mass, the electron, inhibition. Those are the fundamental words which have been evolved in the language exactly as in any human language words for objects and actions have evolved. The sentences are held together by a grammar which tells us what kind of sentence we are allowed to put the unit into. The example that I used was that the gravitational force between two masses is equal to a constant times the product of the masses divided by the square of the distance: that is a sentence $G = k\dfrac{mm'}{r^2}$ that you are allowed to say. You are not allowed to say in the language the same sentence if you put r^3 at the bottom. That is the grammar.

The grammar consists of sentences which are explanations. And then those sentences translate into the real world by a dictionary of translation which tells us how we actually test, confirm, and perceive the fact. For instance, in any specific context, such a sentence translates into some action that takes place. You put two charged electric spheres next to one another in a laboratory, and a movement takes place which is the physical translation of that sentence. And there is a dictionary which says how that is to be translated into the actual world. So much for the language.

Then I asked, Are the things in the language real? Do the inferred units exist? Does the electron exist? Let us take a really highly unlikely particle. Does the neutrino exist? And then, are the explanatory sentences true, is the grammar true? Is Newton's formula a true sentence? Does it really say how masses act? I drew your attention to the fact that though it seemed to be true when it was written (essentially in 1666), it did not seem to be true in 1966 because other explanations had taken its place. How did this come about?

You will recall that I made rather vividly the point that the extraordinary thing that has happened in the last hundred years is that science has kept on revising the explanations and inventing new inferred or fundamental units in the most radical way. I remember Blackett once saying to me when he was reading a paper about a new fundamental particle that something had happened and the paper was now going to be about two new fundamental particles. And he said with some embarrassment, "We really try only to have one new particle *per* paper."

You remember that I drew a chemical equation on the board for Glauber's salts. But let us, in celebration of the fact that Hans Bethe has got the Nobel Prize since I spoke, consider a different sentence:

$$4H^1(\text{hydrogen}) \rightarrow He^4(\text{helium}) + 2\epsilon^+ + 2\beta + 2\gamma$$

This is somewhat simplified (do not actually believe it just the way it stands), but it says essentially that hydrogen becomes helium. Now this involves inferred units: no one has seen a helium atom. But in addition a grammar of explanation was invented by Bethe in the 1930s as to how it went; it went by four steps through carbon.[1] This grammar of explanation was entirely new, and moreover it is *not* the main way that we read the grammar now. Now the dominant equation that creates this is written rather differently, and the steps that Bethe portrayed are no longer regarded as the only ones or even as the most important ones. How has this come about?

Well, I made a radical proposal. I said that it is all due to the fact that none of our explanations can be true, that in some sense there is no ultimate truth accessible to us for the simple reason we have to make a cut in the universe in order to do the experiment at all. We have to decide what is relevant and what is irrelevant. Since I hold that the universe is totally connected, that *every* fact has some influence on every other fact, then it follows that any cut you make at all is a convenient simplification. But in essence it is a distortion, and you are now decoding only a part of the total of sentences. So it is natural that your decoding cannot be right. And it is not surprising that while you keep on getting approximate good answers (the answers are better and better as you progress because you exclude less and less), it is in principle out of the question that we should ever have an ultimate ex-

1. 1) $C^{12} + H^1 \to N^{13} + \gamma$
   $N^{13} \to C^{13} + \beta$
   2) $C^{13} + H^1 \to N^{14} + \gamma$
   3) $N^{14} + H^1 \to O^{15} + \gamma$
   $O^{15} \to N^{15} + \beta$
   4) $N^{15} + H^1 \to C^{12} + He^4$

planation. That would involve setting up experiments in which the whole of the universe was perceived from a God's eye view.

I do not think that there is a God's eye view of nature, that there is a truth, an accessible truth of this kind. The words that I used were that, while the universe is totally connected, we *cannot* extricate ourselves from our own finiteness. And, therefore, we do this decoding by a highly imaginative, creative piece of guesswork. But we finish with something which is only a gigantic metaphor for that part of the universe which we are decoding.

I have said all that again because that is what I have been working up to for three weeks, and today I am going to look at it in a more rigorous context, the context of theorems in mathematics. I am going to be talking about mathematics not as an abstract system, but as a formal language for extracting something from the universe. And the moment I have said that, of course, it is quite clear that we have already made a cut. We are already talking only about things which can be expressed in mathematical equations. But mathematics, of course, has been the most powerful scientific tool ever invented. It has had enormous success, oh, since the time of the Greeks, but especially over the last three hundred years. And if what I have said is true, then it ought to be reflected in the theorems of mathematics. Now mathematics very clearly exhibits this structure: that is, inferred units (for example, ideal points which are not really points) and a grammar of explanation that is called the axiomatic system. It does not exhibit a dictionary of translation, however, unless you decide to apply it to the real world.

Now treating mathematics as if it were made up of concepts or inferred units held together by a grammar is the kind of axiomatic system which originally was invented by the great mathematicians of Greece and of Alexandria. Many of the old difficulties were already known to Euclid. For instance, it was already known in Euclid's time that there was some doubt about what is called the postulate of parallels. (In England, it is sometimes called Playfair's axiom.) Although the doubt was not resolved for over two thousand years, the Greeks knew about it. They did not call the axiom of parallels an axiom, they called it a postulate. It is one of the very interesting things embedded in scientific literature that the Greeks believed the status of some mathematical axioms to be less certain than that of others. They were bothered about the completeness and the consistency of the axioms.

However, everything seemed to be going fine. Late in the 1890s Bertrand Russell wrote a splendid book about the foundations of geometry and became a fellow of Trinity as a result. Then in 1900 he started writing the great work on mathematics which has to some extent formed the whole of our outlook in this century. Let me therefore read to you from Bertrand Russell's autobiography the things he felt in the summer of 1900 when everything seemed wonderful—to be alive was very heaven.[2]

Russell recounts that in the summer of 1900 he went to a congress at which he got to know Peano. Although

2. All quotations are from *The Autobiography of Bertrand Russell: 1872 to World War I* (New York: Bantam Books, 1965), pp. 191–95.

Peano's methods had been known to him, until then he had never really troubled very much about Peano's logical characters. At that time, however, Russell realized that there was a great clue there, and he just went home and spent that summer reading.

> It became clear to me that his [Peano's] notation afforded an instrument of logical analysis such as I had been seeking for years, and that by studying him I was acquiring a new and powerful technique for the work that I had long wanted to do. By the end of August I had become completely familiar with all the work of his school. I spent September [we're speaking of September 1900] in extending his methods to the logic of relations. It seems to me in retrospect that, through that month, every day was warm and sunny.

I think that is a marvelous phrase to give you the impression of how well the work was going. Of course, you never noticed the weather but it all seemed tremendous.

> The Whiteheads stayed with us at Fernhurst, and I explained my new ideas to him. Every evening the discussion ended with some difficulty, and every morning I found that the difficulty of the previous evening had solved itself while I slept. The time was one of intellectual intoxication. My sensations resembled those one has after climbing a mountain in a mist, when, on reaching the summit, the mist suddenly clears, and the country becomes visible for forty miles in every direction. For years I had been endeavouring to analyse the fundamental notions of mathematics, such as order and cardinal numbers.

Suddenly, in the space of a few weeks, I discovered what appeared to be definitive answers to the problems which had baffled me for years. And in the course of discovering these answers, I was introducing a new mathematical technique, by which regions formerly abandoned to the vaguenesses of philosophers were conquered for the precision of exact formulae. Intellectually, the month of September 1900 was the highest point of my life. I went about saying to myself that now at last I had done something worth doing, and I had the feeling that I must be careful not to be run over in the street before I had written it down.

And then he started writing, and he had almost got to the end of the book, which he had hoped to finish by New Year's Day (he counted 1 January 1901 as the beginning of the century, and he wanted to get the book done in the old century). And then he ran into a difficulty:

At the end of the Lent Term, Alys and I went back to Fernhurst, where I set to work to write out the logical deduction of mathematics which afterwards became *Principia Mathematica*. I thought the work was nearly finished, but in the month of May I had an intellectual set-back almost as severe as the emotional set-back which I had had in February. Cantor [this is Georg Cantor] had a proof that there is no greatest number, and it seemed to me that the number of all the things in the world ought to be the greatest possible. Accordingly, I examined his proof with some minuteness, and endeavoured to apply it to the class of all the things there are. This led me to consider those classes which are not members of themselves, and to ask whether the class of such classes is or is not a member of itself. I found that either answer implies its contradictory. At first I supposed that I should be able to overcome the contradiction quite easily, and that probably there was some trivial error in the reasoning. Gradually, however, it became clear that this was not the case. Burali-Forti had already discovered a similar contradiction, and it turned out on logical analysis that there was an affinity [with earlier paradoxes]. . . . It seemed unworthy of a grown man to spend his time on such trivialities, but what was I to do? There was something wrong, since such contradictions were unavoidable on ordinary premises. Trivial or not, the matter was a challenge. Throughout the latter half of 1901 I supposed the solution would be easy, but by the end of that time I had concluded that it was a big job. I therefore decided to finish *The Principles of Mathematics,* leaving the solution in abeyance. In the autumn Alys and I went back to Cambridge, as I had been invited to give two terms' lectures on mathematical logic. These lectures contained the outline of *Principia Mathematica,* but without any method of dealing with the contradictions.

And lest you should think that this disaster in his intellectual life was his only problem, let me read you the next few sentences:

About the time that these lectures finished, when we were living with the Whiteheads at the Mill House in Granchester, a more serious blow fell than those that preceded it. I went out bicycling one afternoon, and suddenly, as I was riding along a country road, I realized that I no longer loved Alys [his wife].

Now I have quoted this fairly extensively because sometimes we think that all the problems in trying to make mathematics exact have arisen in comparatively recent years; say since Gödel in 1931. But of course, Russell's difficulties in May 1901 prove that this is not so.

What Russell had been trying to do was to show that all mathematics (that is, all the grammatical manipulations that we carry on with figures) can be analyzed as straightforward logical operations. You can deal with infinitesimals, you can deal with classes, you can deal with limits, you can deal with group theory—everything will work out. Now what he found was that this was not so. And though he devised ways round it, the very fact that the passages I have been reading to you concern 1900–01, but the *Principia Mathematica* with Whitehead did not begin to be published until 1910, shows that the devices that he invented, the theory of types, did not even satisfy him.

Shortly after that David Hilbert put the thing quite squarely. He said, "We really have to answer the following question. Is it or is it not the case that any sensible mathematical proposition that I can write down can or cannot be proved to be true from the mathematical axioms?" Let me give you a very simple example. Suppose I ask the question, "Is every positive number the sum of four or less squares?" The answer to that question is "Yes, and I can prove it." Supposing I ask the question, "Is every even number the sum of two prime numbers?" The answer to that question is that this was an hypothesis first made by Goldbach more than two hundred years ago, and to this day nobody knows whether it is true or false. Now you might say, "Well, that is ridiculous; you just go on looking at every even number and so you check the theorem." (That is right! I mean that is absolutely what you do.)

All mathematics consists of doing that, but generally speaking, it involves finding shortcuts to doing it. For instance, if you want to prove that every positive number is the sum of four or less squares, you will very soon find that all you have to do is to classify the numbers into primes and nonprimes, then you show first that it is true of all primes, and then that if it is true of any two numbers it is true of their product. You have found a shortcut.

Now the question which Hilbert raised, and which was answered in the negative by my colleagues in the 1930s is this: Are there general procedures for finding shortcuts? That is a good question. If you look at a map there is a procedure for finding a shortcut, but if you look at mathematics, there is no such procedure. And we might take as typical, for instance, the theorem proved by Turing in 1936 which simply says that you cannot be sure when a proof will turn up.[3] You can go on totting up the even numbers, you can go on seeing if they are the sums of two primes, but there is absolutely no way of saying in advance when you are going to come on one which *is not,* so that you have disproved the theorem, or whether you ever are.

It is therefore certain that Hitler's . . . I am so sorry . . . Hilbert's (I do apologize to the memory of a very great man, David Hilbert) that Hilbert's Entscheidungs-

3. A. M. Turing, "On Computable Numbers, with an application to the 'Entscheidungsproblem,'" *Proceedings of the London Mathematical Society* 42 (1937): 230–65.

problem (in the very simple form in which Turing, Alonzo Church, Kline, and so on answered it) is decisively answered. There is no way of making mathematical decisions; there are always theorems whose proofs may or may not turn up. Turing actually did this by mechanizing it. He loved making little machines, and so he invented a device called a Turing machine, and the most important thing that we know is that all mechanisms which, like science, are of this kind are expressible as Turing machines.

However, long before Turing had actually answered that part of the problem, it had first of all been set as an examination question to me and to Max Black in Cambridge in 1930. We did not answer very satisfactorily. But in 1931 a young Austrian called Kurt Gödel published a very remarkable paper called "Part I," ("Part II" has never been published) in which he proved something much stronger and which took the Entscheidungsproblem in its stride.[4] Gödel proved that if you have an axiomatic system of this sort (a formal system, with formal symbols and formal rules of manipulation), there are two things wrong with it. In the first place, if it is consistent, then there are statements that it cannot prove. And not only are there statements that it cannot prove, but there are also *true* statements that it cannot prove.

Now that is much more troublesome than just saying

4. Kurt Gödel, "Über formal unentscheidbare Sätze der Principia Mathematica und verwandter Systeme, Teil I," *Monatshefte für Mathematik und Physik* 38 (1931): 173–89. For a clear, elementary account of Gödel's proof see, E. Nagel and J. R. Newman, *Gödel's Proof* (London: Routledge and Kegan Paul, 1959).

you will never come to them if you go on and on, however long. On the contrary, there are statements which
human mathematicians can actually exhibit and say to you,
"I can prove to you this is true, but the machine cannot."
"All right," you say, "well, feed it into the machine."
Now the machine has an extra axiom which you could not
prove before, and it is well away. No! No! Now I have a
machine of one higher order, a system of one higher order,
but I can construct a sentence of the next higher order
which the machine cannot prove; and so we go on in-
definitely. In other words, if an axiomatic system is consistent, then there are perfectly intelligible statements
which it cannot prove. We do not know whether Goldbach's hypothesis about the sum of two primes is or is
not such a statement, but there are statements that it cannot prove. And we can actually exhibit such statements.

I said, "If an axiomatic system is consistent . . ." If
the system is inconsistent, of course, we are well away
because then it can prove anything. But, unfortunately, it
now no longer distinguishes between true and false propositions. An inconsistent system is perfectly all right; it
can prove the sentences that I can prove. But since it can
prove anything, it is absolutely useless. Let me tell you a
little story about this which is always ascribed to Bertrand
Russell. I did not actually hear him say this, so it may be
a fable. (I do not mean that everything that Bertrand
Russell did not say in my presence is a fable. But there
is obviously a higher incidence of fables among things he
said when I was not there!) Russell is reputed at a dinner
party once to have said, "Oh, it is useless talking about
inconsistent things, from an inconsistent proposition you

can prove anything you like." Well, it is very easy to show this by mathematical means. But, as usual, Russell was much cleverer than this. Somebody at the dinner table said, "Oh, come on!" He said, "Well, name an inconsistent proposition," and the man said, "Well, what shall we say, $2 = 1$." "All right," said Russell, "what do you want me to prove?" The man said, "I want you to prove that you are the pope." "Why," said Russell, "the pope and I are two, but two equals one, therefore the pope and I are one."

So it is useless to deal with inconsistent systems. Yet we have the fact that every closed formal system, if it is consistent, is not able to prove statements that I *can* prove standing outside the system. And we have the additional fact that if the system is inconsistent, it can prove anything, but it is useless. Now what does this say? It says that the reach of all formal systems is limited. When you axiomatize an arithmetical or mathematical system, you automatically impose a limit on it. In the phrase that I have used earlier, you cut the universe in half.

I have been demonstrating this to you only in the case of mathematics. Of course, it does not follow from what I have said that these theorems are true about the real world. It might be that nature is just clever enough to avoid all the pitfalls of these theorems in her actual activity. I believe that there are good grounds for saying that that is not the case. But there also are forms of mathematics which you could use in nature which are not subject to Gödel's theorem. This is not a subject that I want to go into (it is a subject I would love to go into, but it is not a subject that I can go into as part of what I am

saying today). So you must just take it that it is my view
that what I have been saying today about mathematics,
and particularly about arithmetic and theory of numbers
(the very simplest branches of mathematics), is in fact a
model of what I said in the previous lectures about natural systems. It is the axiomatization, it is the formalization of the system which produces the trouble.

Nature is not a gigantic formalizable system. In order
to formalize it, we have to make some assumptions which
cut out some parts. We then lose the total connectivity.
And what we get is a superb metaphor, but it is not a
system which can embrace the whole of nature. We are
really saying that there is no system of axioms which can
embrace the whole of nature, or for that matter the whole
of mathematics. We therefore cannot attain the great wish
that we have had ever since the days of Thomas Hobbes
and Newton: we will never be able to exhibit the whole
of physics one fine day as a gorgeous system with about
six axioms and a few operations, and from that moment
everything would fall into place. You would know why,
for example, flowers that grow at high altitude are often
blue, whereas flowers that grow at low altitude are often
red. Anything that you could ask would follow from the
axiomatic system. That is obviously a hopeless task. What
I have been trying to show is that whether you approach
it in a strictly formal way from the mathematics or in the
more informal way in which I discussed it in the last lecture, you always come to the same conclusion: no formal
system embraces all the questions that can be asked.

In other words, when I said this system is going to consist of true sentences, the fact is that truth is in many

ways the problem. You can prove everything if you no longer distinguish between truth and falsehood. But if you insist on truth and want to do it in an axiomatic system, then there are things which you can show to be true, but which you cannot bring back to the formalism of the system. And if you then force them into the system, then you can show that something else is true which in turn you have to force back in, so that you have an endless regress of axioms that you have to add all the time.

Now we are, roughly speaking, in the same position as Gorgias of Leontium, Plato's least favorite sophist. Plato accused Gorgias of holding that "there is no truth, if there were it could not be comprehended—and if comprehended, it could not be communicated." In some sense, we have this feeling. But of course, we have it only if we ask that absolute systems be constructed which have this simple form. Now the question is, How did it all come about? Why do these theorems occur? And how is it that we are able to prove things to be true when they will not go into the system?

Now Gödel's proof, Russell's original paradox, all these things, all stem from one common root which is inherent in all symbolic languages, including the language we use. This is the problem which dogs all formal systems, the problem of *self-reference;* that is, the language can be used to refer to sentences in the language. Indeed, between 1900 and 1910 Russell tried to forbid this, to say you cannot do mathematics if you do that, and so he invented the theory of types. Of course, no sooner had he invented it than it turned up that you could not do mathematics at all if you obeyed the theory of types. So then he had to put in an axiom of reducibility, which allows a certain amount of self-reference. And by this time everybody was pretty bored.

The problem of self-reference is a classical paradox of Greek literature, in which it is usually referred to as the paradox of the liar, or the paradox of Epimenides the Cretan. Epimenides the Cretan said, "All Cretans are liars." And that is a statement which patently leaves you in a paradox. If all Cretans are liars, then what he is uttering is not true, and therefore he is not a liar at that moment; and if on the other hand, all Cretans are not liars, then what he is saying is true, and therefore all Cretans are liars. To put this into slightly more precise terms, I will read you Bertrand Russell's exposition of this particular paradox. I cut it out of the passage I read to you before, so that we should not get there too fast.

> A contradiction essentially similar to that of Epimenides can be created by giving a person a piece of paper on which is written: "The statement on the other side of this paper is false." The person turns the paper over, and finds on the other side: "The statement on the other side of this paper is true."

And this is why he says in the next sentence, which I did read to you, "It seemed unworthy of a grown man to spend his time on such trivialities, but what was I to do?" I think, myself, that is a very elegant form of the paradox. You think of a piece of paper, and you write on one side that what is written on the other side is untrue, and then you write on the other side that what is written on the other side is true. It is left as an exercise for the student to see that you cannot possibly get out of this paradox. Why is this a paradox? Because to use the phrase, "the statement is" at once puts you into a universe of discourse in which you are no longer using this language to describe things but statements about things. And now you cannot get out.

Indeed, a much more powerful theorem than any of those that I have quoted so far was in fact proved by Alfred Tarski, my favorite among these philosophers because he is a fellow Pole. In 1931, Tarski proved quite simply that all this amounts to saying that there is no complete language of science.[5] If you look at Tarski's proof, it essentially consists in showing that, as soon as you not only exhibit the statements but add to them the statement, "is true," you are in trouble because you are bound to be landed in contradictions like the one which arises in the Epimenides paradox.

It may seem a very long way from this to mathematics and to physics, but it has really been my business in these lectures to take you exactly that way in order to show how enormously closely linked our whole universe of discourse and thought really is. It is of the nature of human language that among the things that it talks about is itself. It is of the nature of human beings that among the things they talk about are themselves. And if you wish to issue a decree that they should not do this, then you move as I did by a slip of the tongue from the universe of Hilbert to the universe of Hitler. Nobody wants to talk in such a way as to be prevented from talking about themselves.

5. A. Tarski, "The Concept of Truth in Formalized Languages" (1931), trans. J. H. Woodger, in A. Tarski, *Logic, Semantics and Metamathematics* (Oxford: Clarendon Press, 1951).

Bless my soul! There would be universal silence. References to yourself are an essential part of our consciousness.

The power of literature, the strength of, say, the lines I quoted in the first lecture from Yeats about her "honey-coloured hair," arises from the fact that we both know what it feels like to be the man in love, and we also know what it feels like to be the woman that is being loved. And the old Greek fable about Tiresias, who had been both sexes at different stages of his life, in some profound way is absolutely true. At any rate our humanity depends on both having in our consciousness a sense of self, and yet also knowing that inside every other person there is a self like ourselves. Now that is very fine to say about literature, and everybody understands it, but the real thunderclap of 1931–36 was to show that you could not do *science* and deny this. Now that really was unexpected. The notion that you really cannot get rid of the paradoxes of self-reference from what seemed to be the ordinary descriptive sentences of science is very strange. The point is that these paradoxes enter into the language of science because we not only want to write sentences in science, we want to say about them that they are true or false. And at once we are back in the universe in which we are using a language in which we refer to ourselves.

In order to say this quite firmly let me just say one more thing. I have told you that Tarski's proof that there is no complete closed scientific language depends on showing that as soon as you introduce the words "is true" you get paradoxes. I told you that Turing's proofs (and the allied proofs of other people) depend on showing that certain things cannot be done in a finite time. I should just tell you what Gödel's proof consists of. What Gödel proved was that no consistent system of axioms can capture all the truths of arithmetic. Any consistent axiomatization is incomplete. The trick he used was to provide a scheme for translating propositions about numbers into propositions about the provability of propositions about numbers. And the crux of his argument is to show how, for any given axiomatization of arithmetic, to produce a proposition about numbers which is true, but which under his ingenious translation scheme "says of itself" that it is not provable from the axioms. So, like the liar paradox, which Gödel cites as one of his sources of inspiration, the result depends crucially upon self-reference.

Now what are we going to do about all this? The answer is straightforward. We have to accept the fact that that is how we do science, that it is essentially a crisis of mechanism in the sense that all science is a Turing machine which is the model of any machine that we can now conceive. But, of course, when there is a crisis of mechanism, you obviously do not get out of your car and start walking. One has, at this stage, simply to admit that mechanism is not a solution to the problem of the universe but a strategy, just as induction and all previous methods of doing science were.

We go on doing science in exactly the same mechanistic way because that is the one strategy by which we make progress. When I first discussed these concepts some years ago, I gave a talk not unlike this, and one of my listeners was Pauling. Pauling got very impatient towards the end of the talk and said to me, "Tell me one operational way in which what you are saying would make me do science differently." To which the answer is, "No, we know no other way of doing science." But it is also quite clear that we now have a conception of what the universe *is* which is different from that which, say, Newton shared with Liebnitz. We have to realize that the total connectivity of nature is something that cannot be imagined in axiomatic systems. To that extent, no proposition that we put, no axiomatic system, no formal language, is ever final. (That is the Incompleteness Theorem.) What is far more important, none of these can possibly be proved to be consistent within the system itself.

I myself think that all explorations of this kind that we do in science are essentially attempts to show that when we run into an inconsistency, we can rearrange the system. As soon as the system runs into a fault, into an inconsistency, the human mind, unlike the machine, has the ability to throw the whole thing away and start building up a new aixomatic system. This is the way general relativity has taken the place of Newton's system, and no doubt something else will take the place of general relativity.

I do not believe that human beings are consistent either, but I think that they have a strategy for coping with inconsistencies which they meet. Let me invent a phrase on the spur of the moment. What human beings have that machines do not have is superb optimism. You know, the thing breaks down, and by Jove, next day they are at it again. You just heard it in the pieces that I read you out of Bertrand Russell, who was struggling with all this and then gets on his bicycle, goes out, and finds he is not in love with his wife. What happened? He gets divorced, he gets married again, he writes the *Principia Mathematica,* and he is still at it. The fact that we are content, when running into this kind of difficulty, to reanalyze the system, to seek a new consistent formulation, is terribly important.

Let us make no mistake about it, the Michelson-Morley experiment in a profound sense actually showed that the Newtonian system (at least as Michelson and Morley conceived it) was inconsistent. You could not give light both the kinds of properties that they wanted, or you could not give the ether that kind of property. In a very profound sense relativity was not just a new physical system, it was a new physical system which was forced by the need to remove an inconsistency. And if you read Einstein's first major paper, he says right at the outset: "I will make the following axioms: that one is not able to detect relative velocity [that's pretty old] and that the velocity of light is constant for every observer however he measures it." [6] Now there was an impertinent remark to make! There was something which threw out the whole of previous physics because, of course, that is an axiom which is absolutely inconsistent with the way we conceived physics before. Well, I must not go on about physics because I really wanted to talk about poetry and connectivity and so on.

Let me say one more thing. I have said of the "inferred units," the theoretical concepts of a science, that they form the links in the system. I have said of the "grammar of ex-

6. Albert Einstein, "Zur Elektrodynamik bewegter Körper," *Annalen der Physik* 17 (1905); trans. M. N. Saha and S. N. Bose, in A. Einstein and H. Minkowski, *The Principle of Relativity* (Calcutta: University of Calcutta Press, 1920), pp. 1–34.

planation," the axiom system of a science, that it is a truth (in so far as there is truth) which we judge by its coherence; whereas through the "dictionary of translation," which relates abstract theorems to specific problems, we judge that truth by its correspondence. And the fact is that once you think of science as that kind of language, then the usual dilemma of philosophy—the coherence theory of truth versus the correspondence theory of truth—disappears. Why? Because you cannot make a theory of scientific explanation which does not involve both, if you believe the universe to be totally connected. And if you believe that, then you have a very good reason for preferring one axiomatic system to another: namely, that it is more richly connected.

If you think for a moment of some systems that have been connected, you will see at once how important this is. Take, for example, the day that Faraday discovered that electricity and magnetism were in fact connected. He had been doing the experiment the wrong way all the time and then one day when he switched off the current, he saw the needle jump. He realized that he had been looking for the connection at the time when the current was going, and that was just the wrong time. (You know, it is the nature of science, it always happens when you are not looking.) At that moment he showed that magnetism and electricity belong to a common system. As a result, the connectivity of the two sets of axioms became higher. He had invented a richer system. And what we have in this sense of richness is essentially a metaphysic which is the equivalent of Occam's razor, or rather the notion that is embedded in Occam's razor, which is that the simpler the hypotheses, the fewer the hypotheses, the more they are to be preferred. And that is saying the same thing as that, if nature is totally connected, then we should prefer those languages or systems which show the highest connection, not because they do in fact show the connections in nature, but because they are coming closest to it.

5

Error, Progress, and the Concept of Time

The program which I set myself, you will recall, was to put into practice the philosophic project that Immanuel Kant once set himself—how is man's view of the world dictated by his biological makeup? In the first lecture I talked particularly about how the senses enter our consciousness. I pointed out that it is *not* true, as eighteenth-century philosophers thought, that our eye is a kind of *camera obscura* which throws a vision of the world somewhere into our heads for us to inspect. This is a childish notion and appropriate for what might be called the childhood of philosophy. But it is obviously silly to think that, instead of looking out at the world, you sit inside your head and you look at a picture of the world which is projected onto your own brain. The whole notion of the world playing itself over again inside our skull, and then there being a self which looks at that, is plainly foolish. The division between man as a receiver of sensations, and man as a thinker, an actor in the world, is mistaken.

When we look at what the eye does, we become aware that it interprets the world from the outset by a process of inference. Perception itself is a mechanism in which sensations are instantly interpreted by an inferential process. I chose the eye as my example because, of course, vision is one of the two main gifts and privileges that man has which put him immensely ahead of the other animals. In the second lecture I concentrated on the second of these gifts, the gift of speech.

I want to pause for a moment to remind you how intimately this is wrapped up with our whole outlook on the world. There is a sonnet by Shakespeare which begins,

> My Mistres eyes are nothing like the Sunne,
> Currall is farre more red, then her lips red,
> If snow be white, why then her brests are dun

I quote this to you because it is so characteristic of how human beings think of the loved object. In line 1 her eyes, in line 2 her lips, in line 3 her breasts. Now, animals are capable of connecting sexual attraction with the secondary sexual organs like the breasts, but the notion of connecting them first with the eyes or with the mouth is, of course, wholly alien to the animal's vision of itself. I think it is very remarkable to think that we think of the loved object as first of all something into whose eyes you look, and then something whose mouth you kiss. And the first of these is connected with the prime importance of vision in human beings, and the second with the even greater importance of speech. Vision is our channel to the outside world, speech is our channel of communication with one another.

In my second lecture I made an analysis of animal language as against human language, and I pointed out that we had invented words where animals have only sentences. We have divided the sentence into words, words which stand for objects or words which stand for actions. And those things are not there in the world, they are the way that we perceive the world. Our consciousness of the world is thing-directed and action-directed because that is how we ourselves speak.

With consciousness comes self-consciousness. We think of ourselves also as objects. And all the paradoxes of science and of literature arise from our attempt to speak simultaneously of ourselves both as knowing selves and as known objects. The second of these has a cardinal importance because by it we identify ourselves with other human beings and indeed with all living things. When Albert Schweitzer talks of "reverence for life," he means that our consciousness is such that because we can equate ourselves with the feeling selves in other animals, we are aware that life is something that goes on inside us all. That was the evolutionary apparatus that I set up in the first and second lectures.

Then in the third and fourth lectures I directed myself to the question, What about science? What about that kind of generalization in which we see the world not only as objects but as classes, as laws, as relations? In the third lecture I presented a view of science as the process of taking the sentences of explanation of how the world works and breaking them into words. And then we invent words like "gravitation" or "electrons," which are just as much inventions as the words "tree" and "love." They are just as real, but they are also just as much something which human beings put into their interpretation of the world. An electron is like a tree, it is there. But if you are asked to define a tree, then you run into the same troubles that you run into when you are asked to define an electron. You can say all the things that it does to your present knowledge, you can say why it seems to you to represent an enormous arrangement of the world; but that is all that you know about it. I will remind you that if I were giving this lecture fifty years from now, the word "gravitation" would be just as old-fashioned to the students of that time as the word "phlogiston" is to us. Relativity has certainly

demoted gravitation as a real explanation, just as Priestley's and Lavoisier's analyses and decoding of chemical
reactions destroyed the word "phlogiston." When Priestley
isolated oxygen and when Lavoisier then said, "Well, all
the things that we have been looking on as phlogistication
and dephlogistication are oxidation reactions," that was a
new decoding in which oxygen played a new part, and
phlogiston was dead. And just so curvature of space-time
for the generation two or three after ours will kill gravitation.

There is no permanence to scientific concepts because
they are only our interpretations of natural phenomena.
Why are they only provisional? Because—and this was
the central point of my third lecture—the part of the
world that we can inspect and analyze is always finite. We
always have to say the rest of the world does not influence
this part, and it is never true. We merely make a temporary invention which covers that part of the world accessible to us at the moment. Who would have thought
when I was an undergraduate that there is an evolution
in the stars, that hydrogen is built up into helium, and
that this is the beginning of a great hierarchy of the elements which at last explains Mendeleef's periodic table.
What has happened? We have suddenly discovered that
parts of the universe which did not seem relevant to the
laboratory, the sun and the stars, are in fact laboratories
themselves. And once we inspected them, we got a larger
integration of the connections in nature which gave us a
new and more subtle interpretation. The world is totally
connected. Whatever explanation we invent at any moment is a partial connection, and its richness derives from

the richness of such connections as we are able to make.

Now in order to establish this in the most direct terms, I devoted my fourth lecture to really a rather difficult subject (which I am happy to be talking about now because even ten years ago it was very hard to get anybody but professional mathematicians to listen to it), the fact that mathematical systems suffer from the same partiality. Gödel, Turing, Tarski all proved this. Gödel proved that you cannot have a complete axiomatization of the whole of mathematics, that every system which you devise is partial and suffers from one great shortcoming. If it is consistent, there are theorems which are true that cannot be proved in it. And Turing showed that every machine that we can devise is like a formal system, and that therefore no machine can do all of mathematics. And Tarski put it even more boldly when he said that no universal language for all of science can exist in all cases without paradox.

Now these theorems are relevant to the subject of this, the fifth lecture, for they tell us something about the brain itself. What is a Turing machine? It is equivalent to any digital computer, that is, to any computer which does all its calculations in discrete steps. Essentially what we have proved is that no such machine can do the whole of mathematics. And by that we mean that we can do a more advanced kind of mathematics than a given machine the moment you show us that machine. Well, that destroys the validity of an old saying, "Show me what a machine cannot do, and I will build you a machine that can do it." The only way that we know to build such a machine is (if I may put the matter very bluntly) to put two human beings of opposite sexes to bed together. Only the human mind can transcend all these machines. Why? Because the human mind is not a digital computer.

Now let me say two things. First of all, how do the paradoxes that tell us all this about digital machines arise? They arise by using the language of the system to describe the system; that is, they arise by what is called "self-reference." Now self-reference, like self-consciousness, is in fact the glory of the human mind. It is the special way in which our language works. Bertrand Russell, who tried to remove self-reference from mathematics in the *Principia,* found very soon that removing it meant you could not do mathematics at all, and that you had to find a device for putting it back. But in any case we would not really want as human beings to do science or mathematics if we were thereby forbidden to think about ourselves, to talk about ourselves, and to compare our feelings from the inside with what we suppose other people to feel whom we only view from the outside. "Cogito ergo sum," (I think therefore I am) is, of course, the basic self-referential statement. Who tells you that you think? How can you even start to make deductions about your thinking process in your own thinking language? And that goes for psychology, it goes for literature, and the striking thing is that it also goes for mathematics and science.

The second point is that this kind of paradox arises from the very nature of knowledge. Tarski showed that any scientific language fails because as soon as you introduce the phrase, "so and so is true," then the introduction of the words "is true" creates a self-reference in the language which gives rise to paradoxes. And you cannot do without those words, you cannot do without "is true." It is of the nature of knowledge, it is of the nature of the cognitive construction of human language that these contradictions occur in it. Now we might naturally ask, Well, what about the brain? How does the brain cope with all this? It is very fine to tell me that no machine can do what the brain can do because the machine is only a digital computer. What is it that the brain can do? Where does the brain fail to be bound by these uncertainties and paradoxes?

There are two things to be said about this. One is that the wholeness of the human being must not be violated by separating the brain from the body. That is what I meant when I said there is no little observer who looks at the *camera obscura* inside your head. This notion arises from problems of consciousness and self-consciousness, divisions between the world and ourselves, and essentially it arises from the whole Cartesian dualism between the mind and the body. What is wrong with this? What is wrong is that if you think of the brain as receiving the information, processing it, and then giving an instruction to the muscle, you have already falsified the whole procedure. There is no nerve without the muscle and no muscle without the nerve in the total animal. This is the same statement as the one I made about the total connection of the world. In terms of the brain and the muscle it can be put very concretely by taking another famous paradox, the great paradox, the Einstein-Rosen-Podolsky paradox in quantum physics.[1] (Please do not be alarmed, but that is what it is called.)

Einstein, as you know, was a delightful person who had

1. A. Einstein, B. Podolsky, and N. Rosen, "Can Quantum-Mechanical Description of Physical Reality Be Considered Complete?" *Physical Review,* vol. 47 (1935).

a special capacity of sometimes treating God as if God were his uncle, and of sometimes treating God as if he were God's uncle. He was always making splendid generalizations, you know, "Raffiniert ist der Herrgott, aber boshaft ist er nicht" (God is cunning but he is not malicious). It is quite untrue: nature is extremely malicious, as every practicing scientist knows. You give her the slightest chance to get out of the experiment by the one trick that you would rather not have to close the door to, and, bang! that is just how the experiment goes wrong. And the most famous of Einstein's sayings about God was that he was not "ein würfelnder Gott" (a God who plays dice).[2] You know, why should God listen to Einstein about what he wants to play at?

Now in order to demonstrate this, Einstein, Podolsky, and Rosen said, "Let us take a closed system in quantum physics and challenge it and then we come out with an answer: this is the state of the system. There is a ψ symbol which describes the state of the system. Now let us take another system to which we give its ψ symbol; now let us join them up, and it suddenly turns out that neither system has the old symbol of ψ attached to it." They say, "Well, that is paradoxical. Why should the total system deny what we had found for the small system?" Well, the answer is that that is just the nature of the universe— whatever partition you make of it gives its own answer, which is not the whole answer.

And it is just the same in the brain. As soon as you

2. See Max Born, "In Memory of Einstein," in *Physics in My Generation* (New York: Springer-Verlag, 1969), pp. 155–65.

separate the brain from the muscle and ask the brain what order it is going to give, you falsify the nature of the brain. We can show this again quite positively. If the brain were separated from the body—and this is the essential fallacy in the Descartes duality of mind and body—if the brain were separated from the body and were fed with the information of the senses and then the output went out to the muscle, then the brain by ordinary quantum physics would have to come up with one of a finite number of answers. Then the brain would be a finite state machine, it would be a digital computer, and it would be enmeshed in all the paradoxes of digital computers. But the point is that you have reached this artificial position because you have put the brain into a box, you have fed the information into this box, and now you have asked it for an answer. As soon as you challenge the box for an answer, then it is bound to print one of a number of digits—you have converted it artificially into a Turing machine.

But if you regard the brain in the body as a totality, then it is exactly what Einstein, Rosen, and Podolsky said —the whole thing comes out with answers which are contained in it, and the brain itself is now no longer acting as a digital computer. The nerve and the muscle are part of a unit. And let me say that all cybernetic approximations to this using a to and fro process fail entirely, because that is only a series of challenges. No, you just have to face the fact that the totality of mind and body forms a unit in which the mind is not a finite state system. The mind, like the hydrogen atom, so long as you do not look at it, is allowed to reach one of an infinite number of answers, and only when action is demanded of it does it come up with a definite answer. But the action now is not an action of the brain—it is an action of the total person.

The most striking way in which to see this is to think for a moment about another of the great paradoxes (this is the lecture of the paradoxes), and that is Heisenberg's paradox about why you cannot measure the momentum and the position of a particle simultaneously. Why? Because you are challenging the particle to print two symbols at the same time. And the particle is not a printing machine. It is not bound by its nature to print symbols. If you challenge it by fixing the position, then it will print an answer to the momentum. If you challenge it by fixing the momentum, or the velocity, then it will print an answer, it will give you the position. But that is not its reality. Its reality is that the whole thing is contained within the particle. As Max Born, Heisenberg's teacher, said, we are trying to press the symbolism of position and momentum beyond what it will really stand by asking of individual electrons what answers they will print to challenges on this.

So we are trying to press the symbolism of, say, algebra beyond what it will stand when we try to say, "Well, every Turing machine does algebra, the mind does algebra; therefore the mind is a Turing machine." As you know that is one of the famous syllogisms that is wrong. Yes, the mind does algebra, and the mind carries out actions and does all kinds of things, but it does not arrive at its actions by actually doing the computations as a finite-state machine does—that is, as a digital computer does. All right, how does it do it? As Einstein used to say, "Meine lieben Damen und Herren . . . !", "Dear ladies and gentlemen, if I knew that, I would know everything!" We none of us know. And what is so exciting about research on the brain at this moment is that although we do not know, we can see how it must go. It is clear that the mind can get this enormous richness because it has a huge number of connections. And these connections are not of the push or pull type, but of some other type in which every connection modulates every other. The result is that the brain must be using some kind of statistical language which is quite unlike human language. The brain does not work inside itself with sentences like "I am hearing you." There is no "I," there is no "you"; that is not how it takes the sentence to pieces. Otherwise it would be a printing machine.

In a Silliman Lecture which I took as my precedent when I accepted the invitation to give these lectures, John von Neumann, who was dying at the time, wrote some of the most splendid sentences he wrote in all his life about this very problem.[3] He pointed out that there were good grounds merely in terms of electrical analysis to show that the mind, the brain itself, could not be working on a digital system. It did not have enough accuracy; or, if it had all that accuracy, it did not have enough memory. There must be some other way. And he wrote some classical sentences saying there is a statistical language in the brain, it is different from any statistical language that we use, we do not know how it goes, but this is what we have to discover. I guess that the discovery will take us the rest of

3. J. von Neumann, *The Computer and the Brain* (New Haven: Yale University Press, 1958).

the life of the universe. But meanwhile, I hope that we shall make some progress. And I think we shall make some progress along the lines of looking for what kind of statistical language would work.

Let me propose an analogy to you. When Robert Boyle invented Boyle's law, he said that if you compressed a gas to half its volume, the pressure would double. In other words, your direct action will give you a pointer reading twice as big. Now all sorts of people after that, chiefly Maxwell and Boltzmann, showed that this was a statistical result of the fact that the gas is full of little atoms rushing about, and that if you halve the volume in which you contain them, then the collisions with the containing walls will give you twice the pressure. In other words, we are seeing what appears to be a unique pointer reading arising as the result of an enormous statistical interplay within the gas. Now I am not proposing that the brain is a gas, you understand. What I am saying is that the nature of the connections inside must be such that when there is input, there is an enormous amount of cross-reference as the result of which there is a certain output. And it is usually the same output.

If you put a man into a psychological laboratory, which Einstein's God forbid, and you say to him, "Bread," he says, "Butter." If he does not say "Butter," you already know there is something wrong with him, he is hiding something. And you can ask him day after day, and he will say, "Butter." But the brain is also able to utter the word "butter" in many settings other than in the psychological laboratory and in response to many things other than this particular inquiry. Moreover, if you change the conditions, the man may no longer say, "Butter." Remember the gas experiment. Boyle's law works fine. When you halve the volume of gas, you double the pressure, *if* you keep the temperature constant. But as soon as you change the temperature, the pointer goes somewhere else. Now the statistical connections within the brain—the number of connections is certainly of the order of ten to at least the tenth or eleventh—the statistical connections within the brain are plainly such (if we take this analogy) that if you alter other conditions and then say "Bread," "Butter" is no longer the response that comes out. You have, according to my analogy, altered the temperature—you have altered another condition, and as a result you get a different response. And these responses must have this statistical character: you feed in a perfectly definite piece of information, you get out a perfectly definite answer, but what goes on inside is not at all a computer-like process. It must be much more like the process which we imagine to go on in a cloud of gas.

Now where do we see this most clearly? When we actually ask ourselves what we are trying to do when we try to press the mind to give exact answers in a symbolism that we have laid down. Why do I require an hour to give this lecture when all I have to say really could go into roughly six sentences? Because I could not utter six sentences which are not so heavily charged with ambiguity that no one in the end would get the picture that I am trying to formulate. Most of human sentences are in fact aimed at getting rid of the ambiguity which you unfortunately left trailing in the last sentence. Now I believe this to be absolutely inherent in the relation between the symbolism of language (that is, an exact symbolism) and the brain processes that it stands for. It is not possible to get rid of ambiguity in our statements, because that would press symbolism beyond its capabilities. And it is not possible to get rid of ambiguity because the number of responses that the brain could make never has a sharp edge because the thing is not a digital machine. So we have to work with the ambiguities. And nearly all discussions about Turing's theorem or about poetry always come back to this central point about ambiguity. One of my fellow mathematicians, William Empson, who did mathematics with me at Cambridge, turned to poetry and at once published a book called *Seven Types of Ambiguity,*[4] which the English students here will know—it is still a kind of minor bible, but a bible written by a mathematician, never forget that.

Ambiguity, multivalence, the fact that language simply cannot be regarded as a clear and final exposition of what it says, is central both to science and, of course, to literature. Why to science? We have just seen it—we have just seen that whenever you try to press the symbolism to do more than it can do, you fail. Why? For the same reason that you cannot make a single general statement about anything in the world which really is wholly delimited, wholly unambiguous, and divides the world into two pieces.

You cannot say anything about gravitation which excludes it from the space-time in which it is now embedded; you cannot say anything about a table or a chair which

4. London: Chatto & Windus, 1930.

does not leave you open to the challenge, "Well, I am using this chair as a table." Kids do it all the time, "I am using this chair as a table, it is now a table or a chair." If that seems silly to you, I will remind you of a phrase I read you from Bertrand Russell last week. "It seemed unworthy of a grown man to spend his time on such trivialities, but what was I to do?" It is very hard to ask yourself, Why do I have to worry about whether I can really define a table so that every object in the world is now classified as being a table or not a table? Well, the world is not like that. For one thing, the world does not consist simply of an endless array of objects and the word "table" was not invented in order to bisect the universe into tables and non-tables. And if that is true of "table," it is true of "honor," and it is true of "love," and it is true of "gravitation," and it is true, of course, of "mass" and "energy" and everything else.

Now this was really demonstrated for the first time by my teacher Frank Ramsey, who showed that if a scientific system was so completely precise that you could replace every word in it, such as "electrons," by the totality of all observations on the electron, then you could never discover anything new.[5] And of course, Ramsey's theorem is really equivalent to all the Tarski-Turing theorems in essence because it says that if you push the symbolism even in a word like "mass" so that you say, as operationists do well, mass is everything you do when you weigh

5. F. P. Ramsey, *The Foundations of Mathematics and Other Essays,* ed. R. B. Braithwaite (New York: Harcourt, Brace, 1931), pp. 212–36.

the mass, you are never going to discover that mass and
energy are interchangeable. You have closed the system
to new discoveries. What I really have to say in all this
is contained in those words.

Science is an attempt to represent the known world as
a closed system with a perfect formalism. Scientific discovery is a constant maverick process of breaking out at
the ends of the system and opening it up again and then
hastily closing it after you have done your particular piece
of work. You would like yours, of course, to be the last
discovery. But alas—or, I prefer to say, happily—it is not
so. It is in the nature of all symbolic systems that they can
only remain closed so long as you attempt to say nothing
with them which was not already contained in all the ex-
perimental work that you had done. If you want a closed
system (which is what Newton's contemporaries hoped
that he had achieved), then you must believe that the
whole world has now been described and that everything
else is just a kind of trivial embroidery. For example, you
have now explained everything in biology about human
beings, you have a few minor things to explain, like why
some people have curly hair, some people have straight
hair, some people have no hair at all, but that is all that
remains to be done. Well, neither biology nor physics nor
chemistry nor any other subject is like that.

What distinguishes science is that it is a systematic attempt to establish closed systems one after another. But
all fundamental scientific discovery opens the system again.
The symbolism of the language is found to be richer than
had been supposed. New connections are discovered. The
symbolism has to be broadened. Symbolism, language,

scientific formulae here are all synonymous. What opens it? That function of the brain which in fact is not the function of a digital computer.

I have a great many friends who are passionately in love with digital computers. They are really heartbroken at the thought that men are not digital computers. Since most of them are men, they would like to make an exception of women, but so far as the male brain is concerned, they would love to feel that it is a digital computer. And that seems very strange to me. They would love to feel that the end of science is only just over the horizon. Why they are so keen to work themselves out of a living I do not understand!

The endless progress of science, of course, arises exactly from the fact that you can go on doing mathematics which the machine could not do. You can go on working at whether the system is consistent or not. And as I said in the fourth lecture, when you come on a profound discovery like the Michelson-Morley experiment, which is really essentially an inconsistency in the system, then you reorganize the whole thing. And that reorganization is the central act of imagination.

The act of imagination is the opening of the system so that it shows new connections. I originally put this idea in *Science and Human Values* [6] when I said that every act of imagination is the discovery of likenesses between two things which were thought unlike. And the example that I gave was Newton's thinking of the likeness between the thrown apple and the moon sailing majestically in the sky.

6. Harmondsworth: Pelican, 1956; rev. ed., New York: Harper & Row, 1965.

A most improbable likeness, but one which turned out to be (if you will forgive the phrase) enormously fruitful. All acts of imagination are of that kind. They take the closed system, they inspect it, they manipulate it, and then they find something which had not been put into the system so far. They open the system up, they introduce new likenesses, whether it is Shakespeare saying, "My Mistres eyes are nothing like the Sunne" or it is Newton saying that the moon in essence is exactly like a thrown apple. All those who imagine take parts of the universe which have not been connected hitherto and enlarge the total connectivity of the universe by showing them to be connected.

Now my official subject today was "error, progress, and the concept of time." I had proposed to take time as an example of a particular concept which had, through successive generations, been opened in this way—changing first from absolute Newtonian time to the time of relativity, then involving the whole question of cosmic time, and in particular evolutionary time. I shall not try to give you a thumbnail sketch of time, but there is one point that I want to pick out: In my concept of time, which is largely connected with evolutionary time, the notion that errors are made by nature, that replication is not perfect, is central. Evolution is built up by the perpetuation of errors. It runs counter to the second law of thermodynamics by promoting the error to the new norm so that the second law now works on the error, and then a new error is built up. That is also central to all inductive acts and all acts of imagination. We ask ourselves, "Why does one chess player play better than another?" The answer is not

that the one who plays better makes fewer mistakes, because in a fundamental way the one who plays better
makes more mistakes, by which I mean more imaginative
mistakes. He sees more ridiculous alternatives. If any of
you play chess you may have sat in front of the board
with a published diagram and then refused to look at the
next move, saying, "Well, what crazy thing did he do
now?" The mark of the great player is exactly that he
thinks of something which by all known norms of the
game is an error. His choice does not conform to the way
in which, if you want to put it most brutally, a machine
would play the game.

Therefore, we must accept the fact that all the imaginative inventions are to some extent errors with respect to
the norm. Nothing is worth doing which is not this mad
maverick kind of change. But these errors have the peculiar quality of being able to sustain themselves, of being
able to reproduce themselves.

Nor must we decry the fact that we do all kinds of
experiments, and every so often we are wrong—more
often wrong than right. More scientific theories are wrong
than right. Of course, the wrong ones do not get published so often. But never confuse the process of exposition with the process of discovery. You see, unfortunately,
the B-movies showing Paul Muni discovering some anti-
something or other always represent the scientists at the
moment of triumph, with the notion that there it is, here
is the discovery. Well, that is not how the discovery is
made. The discovery is made with tears and sweat (at any
rate, with a good deal of bad language) by people who
are constantly getting the wrong answer. And it is not

possible to eliminate it because that is the nature of looking for imaginative likenesses. You are always looking for a likeness and nine out of ten of the likenesses you are looking for are not there. So, of course, more bad science is produced than good and more bad works of art are produced than good ones. The difference is only that most scientists take care not to exhibit *their* bad work.

Progress is the exploration of our own error. Evolution is a consolidation of what have always begun as errors. And errors are of two kinds: errors that turn out to be true and errors that turn out to be false (which are most of them). But they both have the same character of being an imaginative speculation. I say all this because I want very much to talk about the human side of discovery and progress, and it seems to me terribly important to say this in an age in which most nonscientists are feeling a kind of loss of nerve.

I was up at Berkeley eighteen months ago when all the boys were saying "We do not want to be computer cards." I quite agree—nobody wants to be an IBM card, and all those remarks about "do not fold or otherwise mutilate, this is a human being" were absolutely just. But that has nothing to do with the nature of science. You must remember that by the time science becomes a closed—that is, computerizable—project, it is not science anymore. It is not in the area of the exploration of errors. I want very much to transmit to you—scientists as well as nonscientists—the feeling of adventure, of exploration, in this exactly because we are all the time pushing the boundaries of the closed scientific system into an area which is full of pitfalls and errors.

And I object to trying to close the system in literature as much as I object to it in science. I think that Sartre's *Huis Clos*—Sartre's *No Exit*—is a terrible play. I do not mean terrible as a play but terrible in the philosophy that it regards as dictating boundaries to human beings. It is terrible for exactly the same reason that I think that any scientist who really believes that what he is doing is a mechanical process is in a terrible state of mind.

If we ask "Why do we know more now than we knew ten thousand years ago, or even ten years ago?" the answer is that it is by this constant adventure of taking the closed system and pushing its frontiers imaginatively into the open spaces where we shall make mistakes. But we also know something of the laws and responsibilities by which that investigation is bounded. My sixth and last lecture will deal with this. It is called "Law and Individual Responsibility," and I mean by the word "law" just what the State Department means, not a law of nature, but a state law. Because I think the questions of what we mean by natural law and what we mean by human law are intimately bound up with science.

6
Law and
Individual
Responsibility

On this slightly maudlin occasion, the last of six lectures, I want to talk about the practice of science, first as an individual activity and then as a social activity. I am going to speak for a little while about the kind of person who succeeds in science. Then I will make a brief transition between what might be called the personality of the scientist and the community of scientists into which he has to fit. I shall then talk about the community of scientists, what holds it together, how it works, and why it has had spectacular success, which (in the comparatively short time between, let us say, 1666, when Newton was startled to see the apple fall, and 1967) has made it the largest single factor in our social life. And finally, I shall speak about the place of science in our society today, not as a technical activity, nor even as a search for knowledge, but as the kind of ethical activity it is. When I gave this lecture its title, it was because I wanted to talk very clearly about the ethical conditions which have made the practice of science successful and, indeed, possible.

Let me begin by talking about the scientist as a person. In the fourth of my lectures I told you a story about Linus Pauling. I said that I had given a talk to a small group of scientists roughly on the lines of that lecture, namely, about the limitations inherent in all axiomatic scientific systems in what in the last lecture we learned to call closed systems. And I told you how, as I came near the end of the lecture, Pauling became more and more restless, and how, as soon as I had finished, he said to me, "Operationally speaking, as a practicing scientist, how does all this affect me? How should my practice as a scientist be changed by the fact that you tell me convincingly that

mechanism is not the answer to the world as it is put together?" And I said blandly and sweetly, "Not at all. What
we have really proved is that mechanism is not an ultimate explanation of the world, but it is the only strategy
that we know for penetrating the laws. And you go right
on doing it." But now I must tell you the rest of the story,
because then Pauling said to me, "OK, why should I care?
Why bother me with all this abstruse stuff about how the
world is really put together?"

I cannot pretend to recall my reply verbatim—in any
case I am sure that the form in which I will tell it to you
will be more flattering to me than what I really said. But
I did rather feel as T. H. Huxley felt on that famous day
in 1860 at the British Association in Oxford when Bishop
Wilberforce had the folly to ask Huxley whether he
claimed descent from the monkey on his father's or his
mother's side, and Huxley said to his neighbor before he
got up to reply, "God has delivered him into my hands"
(a piece of piety which I must say I am sorry that Bishop
Wilberforce did not overhear). So I said on this occasion
to Pauling, "Well, that is a very strange thing for you to
say, because you of all people are a man who has demonstrated that a scientist is not merely a man who makes
profound imaginative discoveries, but a man who regards
the world as a whole. Here you are, the only man in the
world who has actually won two Nobel Prizes, one for
chemistry and the other for what?—for peace, if you
please. And you ask me why the change in the world picture of science should affect scientists. You, Pauling, are
the personal demonstration of the fact that a scientist is
a complete person and that he can no more talk about

chemistry without thinking about peace than he can talk about peace without thinking about chemistry." Now I am happy to say that Pauling said absolutely nothing in reply.

There is, of course, a reply. There are scientists much given to thinking of themselves as machines, and they would reply: "Oh, no, no. What I do for peace is a deduction from my chemistry. I have these convictions about peace because I am a scientist." I do not share this view. I do not think that you can prove that peace is desirable in any kind of mathematical system which avoids all the difficulties of Gödel's theorem and so on. If you want peace, if you want any particular form of human community, it is not because science has proved it to be desirable, but because it is to you part of the same world picture that science gives you. And a man like Pauling who has crazy ideas about world peace and crazy ideas about chemistry is, of course, the scientific personality. In spite of all their attempts to look and behave like computers, scientists are maverick personalities. It is not possible constantly to face the world with the idea that the explanation which you have just been told is sure to be wrong unless you are a very questioning, a very challenging kind of person.

I once addressed, on a Christmas day many years ago, on behalf of the United Nations, an audience of about two thousand school children in London. As on this occasion, I knew in general what I was going to say, but I did not know exactly what I was going to say, and in a moment of abandon I said to them: "This is how the world goes, you are going to have to make it different, you are going to have to stop listening to your parents. If you go on obeying your parents, the world will never be a better place." And at that moment twenty newspaper men representing the European press got up from the front row and rushed for the telephone boxes. And by the time I got home one of the more adventurous correspondents from Geneva had actually phoned my daughter, then aged seven, at school in order to ask her whether she was encouraged to disobey her parents at home.

But that is what we mean. And indeed, if I may lapse for a moment into my views on sociology, one of the reasons why, on the whole, women have had difficulty so far in making very good scientists is that they are not contrary enough. Happily time will cure all that. Time will produce belligerent, contrary, questioning, challenging women as it has produced belligerent, contrary, questioning, challenging men. None of us cares for them, it is always a nuisance to have them in the laboratory. Read Watson's account of what Bragg thought of having Francis Crick in the laboratory in Cambridge, and you will see how the best of scientists still finds it very awkward to have even a brash young man, who is going to be just as good as he, going round contradicting everything that the great man says.[1]

Now it is very important to recognize this kind of personality because, of course, it makes the changes in society. We have been for some hundreds of years a society directed towards change. And it is people like that who are the catalysts, the stimulators, the creators of change. And they are this as complete personalities.

1. J. D. Watson, *The Double Helix: A Personal Account of the Discovery of DNA* (London: Weidenfeld & Nicolson, 1968).

Senator McCarthy used to be troubled by the fact that he was constantly faced by good scientists who were not in his opinion good citizens. And he would constantly utter rather plaintive little cries, the burden of which was roughly, "Mr. Einstein (not that he ever saw Einstein, but let us take a neutral name), why cannot you invent relativity and keep out of politics?" He did not mean that, however, he meant, "Mr. Einstein, why cannot you invent relativity without at the same time voting for my opponent?" That is what people usually mean when they advise you to keep out of politics. To that, of course, people like Einstein have always had to reply, "If I were not a very awkward character, I would not have thought of relativity in the first place." You do not invent a new world system by being satisfied with what other people have told you about how the world works. And that dissatisfaction goes through and through, and it makes a complete personality. The scientist is as completely involved in the whole of his work as any poet or artist and, I suppose, bank manager or truck driver. If he does the job well, it is because it is him. Einstein used to play the violin, execrably, I am glad to say. But he played it and he did not play it the way a tennis player goes out to take twenty minutes of exercise. He did not play it in order to exercise anything. He played it as part of the human being that he was.

Now all this only makes sense, of course, if you accept the fact that science is not a finished enterprise—that knowledge is not a finished enterprise, that literature is not a finished enterprise. To go looking for the truth only has a point if the truth has not already been found. And naturally if you suppose that the truth is a thing, that you could find it the way you could find your hat or your umbrella, then none of this makes sense, then you just look for a good finder. But that is not how truth is found. It is not how knowledge is created, and it is not how it works to quicken and leaven and create social change. The kind of questioning personality that I am describing is one who is appropriate to our changing society only because he is the self-correcting mechanism. He is the thermostat built into the system. He is the man who says, "That is not right, we will try it another way." Science is essentially a self-correcting activity. But more important, scientists are people who correct the picture of the moment with another one, as a natural evolution towards a "true" picture of the world. We have spoken enough about truth to know that we are not going to get a final picture of the world. Nobody is going to find the truth one fine day, as I say, like a hat or an umbrella.

Now a good deal of attention has been given to scientists as human beings before now, and Roe has written an excellent book about it.[2] And this kind of heroism, the heroism of being a contrary man is well known to us all, if only from the cinema. I want to turn your attention now to the community of scientists. Because you see, what has made science successful as a social leaven over the last three hundred years is its change from the practice of individuals, however great their ingenuity, to a communal enterprise.

2. Anne Roe, *The Making of a Scientist* (New York: Dodd, Mead & Co., 1953).

Leonardo da Vinci was born in 1452. He died in 1519. No scientific society existed at that time; neither Shakespeare nor Galileo had yet been born. And one reason why immensely prolific, vivid, imaginative, and inventive brains like Leonardo's failed to make any impact on the body of science was that there were no colleagues. There were colleagues in painting, and they undoubtedly had an influence which produced more and better paintings than we should otherwise have. And now that there have been so many scientists and so few painters, I am well content to let Leonardo da Vinci alone. But I do want you to see that even that tremendous mind could not work in isolation.

This is a particularly crucial point because, in a way, everything that I have been saying about the maverick personality so far is really true of all creative minds. You know, Shakespeare and Goethe were just as troublesome to their teachers at school as Leonardo and, say, Rutherford. The creative personality is always one that looks on the world as fit for change and on himself as an instrument for change. Otherwise, what are you creating for? If the world is perfectly all right the way it is, you have no place in it. The creative personality thinks of the world as a canvas for change and of himself as a divine agent of change.

But, you see, it is rather puzzling why on the whole science took off about three hundred years ago and has been so very successful in expanding its kind of knowledge when on the whole the same cannot be said of the arts. Do not let me appear to denigrate the arts. I believe that we live in a period of literary and artistic creation quite as great as any of the past. And I think that this is just the way history works. If you are at a moment of obviously enormous scientific inventiveness (such as this century), then the world of the arts takes fire as well. But it takes fire in a different way. There is not this sense that somehow pop art is obviously much better than *The Virgin of the Rocks*. Whereas it is perfectly clear that the elucidation of the DNA molecule is a great deal better than those pictures of the homunculus which they used to draw in the fifteenth century.

Now this is because science is and can be practiced as a communal activity. The community of scientists has a special strength. You can see this very easily. Since so many Nobel Prize winners have been announced over the last weeks let me draw your attention to one very obvious thing. If you look at a list of the people who since 1900 have won Nobel Prizes in physics, biology and medicine, chemistry, there is hardly a name which you would not recognize and highly respect. But, alas, if you look at the list of the people who have won the Nobel Prize for literature during the sixty odd years that it has been awarded, it really makes rather sad reading. When I was a boy the Nobel Prize for literature was awarded one year to a lady called Selma Lagerlof. Now I doubt whether more than one or two of you have ever read a book by Selma Lagerlof. I suppose I could find more obscure names, and I could also find some very great names that were not awarded the prize. Clearly there is much more uncertainty involved in the awarding of literary prizes.

Now I make this comparison only in order to point out

something about the judgments of scientists as a community that has nothing to do with whether scientists are being better judges or whether literary critics are good or bad. It has to do with the fact that in the practice of science everybody knows what everybody else's work is. How has this been possible? Of course, it is very simple. In the end you cannot propose a scientific theory unless it conforms to a certain sanction of fact. Now, it is true of literature, it is true of painting, that it has to conform to some sanctions of how human beings think and feel and act, but such sanctions are not so easily exhibited as the physical facts of science. If I write a paper and it goes to China and Czechoslovakia and South America and Los Angeles everybody in all these places who reads it believes that I am telling the truth as I see it. Nobody assumes that what I am saying is true. It is not given to us to know what is true in that sense. But everybody knows that I write the scientific paper on an implicit, unwritten understanding among scientists that it can be absolutely believed to be what I believe.

Now, unhappily, that kind of simple sanction simply does not exist in any other subject. I shall return to this when I talk about the influence of the scientific ethic, but it is clear that if I were writing a political pamphlet and sent it to China, Czechoslovakia, South America, and Los Angeles, nobody would suppose for a moment that I had written it with the express purpose of putting down what I believed to be true and nothing else.

Now I draw your attention to the fact that this adherence to the literal truth works in detail, not in the large. I am not allowed to say, "I think the theory of relativity is true, I think it would be a splendid thing for everybody to believe it, why do I not cook the evidence just a little so that it will appear to be true? Why do I not select the facts in favor of it and suppress the facts against it?" Now this is absolutely crucial: scientists never discuss *ends,* they only discuss *means,* the steps by which you get from today's knowledge to tomorrow's knowledge. It is wonderful when a man produces a grand theory and one has a new direction to work toward, a new end. But the means have got to be absolutely honest. You cannot say, "It would be a good thing if I were in charge of the nation's science next year, it would certainly be a better thing than if somebody else were in charge, and therefore it would be a good thing if I got all my fellow scientists to say that this discovery or that discovery of mine was true when, in fact, I know it to be false." There are spectacular cases of this kind, as you know. There have been scientists in whose laboratories some forgery was carried out (Kammerer is the best known example) and who committed suicide because life was intolerable in those circumstances.[3]

Of course, something came into European civilization at the time of the Renaissance which in general inclined our society this way. I told you the story of how Kepler (by way of Nicholas of Cusa) probably heard about God's love making all things attract one another from a man who went by the name of Dionysius the Areopagite, who claimed to be a Church father, but who in fact was later found to be a fifth-century forger. Well, unhappily, between 1500 and 1600, a number of such forgeries turned

3. Arthur Koestler, *The Case of the Midwife Toad* (New York: Random House, 1973).

up in very important Church documents.[4] And the men of Florence and Milan were astonished to think that there had been a time in the history of the Church when it was thought that in order to convert the faithful to the glory of God it was all right to put forged documents into the records.

Now so far, I have been speaking only of the scientific enterprise as taking its strength from the fact that everybody can believe what everybody else says. But in the end, after all, what is science discovering except what is the case? How do we build norms of conduct on that? And I want now to turn to the norms of conduct in the scientific community that arise from this.

It is basic to the concept of truth as practiced in science that it is an absolute command in every detail. There is no distinction between good means and good ends. You are only allowed to employ perfectly honest means. This is what puts you in a position of special trust. And this is a deeply ethical principle. You see, for a long time past there has been an assumption that the findings of science are neutral. "What is" simply is the case, and how can you get an "ought" out of that? The argument was probably first put forth by G. E. Moore in the *Principia Ethica,* but it is probably much older than that and goes back at least to the eighteenth century. But the argument is that from what is you cannot draw any information as to how you ought to act. And the transition from "is" to "ought" is usually called the naturalistic fallacy. I do not accept this.

4. The fraud of Dionysius the Pseudo-Areopagite was one of the impostures and forgeries exposed by the Italian humanist Lorenzo Valla (1404–57).

There are three different arguments against the naturalistic fallacy. Two due to other people and one due to me. I will briefly deal with those due to other people. The first simply says—and rightly—that every time you know something about the world there are certain forms of conduct which are obviously ridiculous. Once you know that gravity goes down and not up, it is ridiculous to build buildings in which you assume that it goes up. Once you know how gravitation works outside the earth, there are certain forms of spaceships which you will not build. Once you know that there are two sexes, then certain forms of behavior become pointless. (Perhaps that is not a very wise remark. At least, certain forms of behavior become pointless for the community as a whole.) I think this is perfectly sensible. I think that it is perfectly true that the more we know, the stronger we are in our choices. It is not true that because our choices become narrower, they become weaker. On the contrary, we have a firmer ground for making choices. However, I think this is not a very important argument.

A more interesting argument, which has been put forward largely by Waddington, is: "Well, human beings are the way they are [after all, the whole point of these lectures that I am giving is this is how human beings are] and we ought to act as human beings are." I think that is a good argument. I think it is very important to find what human beings are really capable of and to act accordingly. I think it is a perfectly fair criticism to say that the guards in concentration camps acted like beasts. (Though I must just say in fairness to beasts that you cannot find beasts who act like that. It is very specific to human conduct to be able to be as bestial as that.) I think it can be held that the more we know about our evolutionary history, about our potential as human beings, the more clear it becomes that we have become the way we have because of certain gifts and that it is right that we should practice those gifts.

However, I think that one needs neither of these metaphysical arguments in face of the last argument, which is my own. You all know it since the one book of mine that everybody has read is *Science and Human Values* and I advanced it there for the first time. This argument says simply that you cannot know what is true unless you behave in certain ways. What is the good of talking about what is, when in fact you are told how to behave in order to discover what is true. "Ought" is dictated by "is" in the actual inquiry for knowledge. Knowledge cannot be gained unless you behave in certain ways.

The most interesting example of this is, of course, the Nazi doctors in the concentration camps and the Nazis in general. They found themselves in an extraordinary paradox. They knew the ultimate truth, they knew that Aryans were better than anybody else so they knew that relativity could not be true, because after all it had been proposed by Einstein. They were not scholarly enough to be able to remember that Poincaré had made a very similar proposal. When Heisenberg was actually foolish enough to give a speech to his students saying, "You must read relativity, never mind whether Einstein was a Jew or not," Himmler actually had Heisenberg investigated. And, because in this kind of totalitarian state everything is done by nepotism, fortunately Himmler's aunt knew a cousin of Heisenberg's, so he was OK.

But you see their dilemma. On the one hand they were

addicted to the founding principle of the modern state, which is that knowledge brings you power; and on the other hand they were not willing to accept the fact that you can only gain knowledge by being truthful. For example, if you put forward a fable that Negroes are more nearly related to chimpanzees than Hitler is, then you sap the foundations of science. And sooner or later the whole thing comes tumbling about your ears, because if you also want to build a policy, say just about genetics, on this kind of false premise, it cannot be done. A basic reason why no discovery of importance was made by the Nazis throughout the war, why the doctors in the concentration camps with all their opportunities made such a pitiful show of nonsense, was because Nazi scientists were caught in a dreadful paradox; they only knew one way to get knowledge, but that was exactly the way that was forbidden to them.

Once you regard truth (truth in detail) as the cement of the scientific community, then it follows at once that people have got to behave so that the truth shall be apparent. You see, it is very fine for all of us in this room to talk as if we could all have invented something simple, like the steam engine, had the necessity arisen. You know perfectly well that you could not. Imagine yourself for a moment, actually in the unhappy position of being cast away on a desert island among a lot of Trobrianders. You say to them, "We have marvelous things," and they say, "Well, what?" And you say, "Well, a bicycle." So they say, "OK, make us a bicycle." You would not know how to begin to make a bicycle. Do you know how a gear works? Can you even remember how the chain goes? Do you know what kind of metals you need for it?

Benjamin Huntsman spent the whole of his life building what has since become the metallurgic industry of Sheffield in order to make a better watch spring, because he was not satisfied with the way in which watches went when he was a boy. Nobody who now makes a watch spring of this kind gives a thought to Benjamin Huntsman. But it is out of the individual work of such people that science is made. Now Huntsman would not become a fellow of the Royal Society because as a Quaker he despised all worldly honors. He kept his formulas a great secret. Indeed, he buried specimens of his work that were not up to his standard, and other people in Sheffield dug them up and made perfectly good steel that he did not think good enough. But the watch, in the end, if you think of it, is made out of the communal work of such people.

And if you can make a watch today, it is because you can actually believe what Robert Hooke said about the escapement, what Huygens said about the escapement, and so on and so on. And that is true of every scientific theory. You cannot take the simplest statement in science without having to believe a lot of people. I know an awful lot of biologists and there are many subjects about which I would not believe a word they said. But when they start talking about how DNA is put together, then I know that they are telling the truth. We could not work without that tradition, which started back in 1660 when scientific papers really began as personal letters from one friend to another. That has been the quickening life force in science which has made it possible for people to have an absolute trust in one another's statements. So that from the attempt to find the "is," for example, exactly how many seconds there are in a year, we are forced to the "ought"; namely, you ought to tell me how to make a good watch spring, and I ought to be able to believe you.

I have told you that I said all this in 1953 in *Science and Human Values.* Many of you have read it, so I am slightly embarrassed about repeating the argument, but if you have not I will ask you to turn to the argument because I then go on to show how the other values derive from truth. There are the personal values—respect, sensitivity, tolerance—without which science could not be carried on. They are the "is" values, the values of the man working by himself. And then there are the communal values, the "ought" values—honesty, integrity, dignity, authenticity—which bind the scientific community together. And on the basis of this, science has been able for three hundred years to change completely (as I have told you several times) practically every fifty years. Nobody is shot, nobody is *gleichgeschaltet,* nobody is liquidated. People whose theories have been wrong retire full of honors. Somebody was talking to me this very afternoon about Patrick Blackett's theory that magnetism is due to rotation. I remember when the theory came out, I remember that it has not worked. Patrick Blackett is now president of the Royal Society, and nobody says to him, "Come on, you are no good, you made a mistake." But on the other hand, if he had been going about ever since then pretending he had not made a mistake, making ingenious experiments to say he had not made a mistake, bribing his colleagues to give testimonials about what a good fellow he was, he would not be president of the Royal Society, I do assure you.

If you are going to make what science has been—a

stable body of knowledge which at any given moment is closed and yet is always changing—and if that is really going to be dynamic, yet stable, then you have to build in the conditions and the safeguards for absolute integrity. The society of scientists, the community of scientists, has this advantage, that from the moment we enter it, we all know that fifty years from now, most of the things we learned here will turn out not to have been quite right. And yet that will be achieved without enormous personal dramas. It will be achieved by giving due honor to the people who take the steps, the steps that turn out to be wrong as well as the steps that turn out to be right. You have to build this into the social relations if the society is to be able to maintain itself in the face of change, otherwise you get a rigid totalitarian society of the kind Plato wanted to build, Hitler wanted to build, Mussolini wanted to build, Stalin wanted to build. And all that I know about all these societies is that I have seen Hitler die, and Mussolini die, and Stalin die, while the societies in which I was fortunate to be brought up have on the whole sustained themselves without the enormous human loss of those others.

Having said this, it would be timid of me not to say something about the impact of this aspect of science into our society. We, we the people in this city and in the world now, are living for the first time in what is essentially a community penetrated through and through by the scientific outlook. And the scientific outlook is inseparable from the scientific ethic. I read in the paper four days ago that nuns have the longest expectation of life of any group in this country. Their average expectation of life is seventy-seven years. Now I believe this absolutely, not because I read it in the paper but because I recognize the name of the man who published the findings. I am not, therefore, tempted to be a nun. It does not in itself tell me anything about being a nun. Some people may be influenced by such considerations, among others. But the very fact that such questions are asked and answered shows how we are penetrated in all respects by this kind of outlook and the fact that we place absolute trust in it. We do not therefore say, "Oh well, now we have to believe in Roman Catholicism or we have to disbelieve in Roman Catholicism." We just say, "Well, that is it. Interesting, is it not? You should not eat so much. Or you should not smoke, perhaps."

We are living at the moment in history when the scientific ethic comes through everything. The notion is that you can believe it, it is in the paper, it is not a piece of propaganda by one religious sect or another, it has been said by a scientist in a serious publication. If, on the other hand, this kind of thing had been put out by some sectarian agency, we would not have believed it.

I think that at present there is quite a crisis in the history of politics and government. I think that it is a very difficult time to have governments run by people who are really too old to have quite this spirit. All the arguments about wars and credibility gaps and so on in the end come down to this: that we are all growing up in university communities, intellectual communities in general, with a feeling that we trust people to say just what they think. We believe that they will tell the truth, we believe that they will organize society so that honesty, integrity, dignity, and so on are respected. And then we are very disappointed when it happens not to be so. When I meet university students, I am conscious of the fact that they do not think that this is a credibility gap, they just think it is a hypocrisy gap. They just think that in the political community, in the relations between states, you, the elders, are allowed to practice a form of hypocrisy, which they are not allowed to practice within the hallowed halls of universities.

As you know, I am not an American. (Listening to me, it must slowly have dawned on you.) And there are some American institutions which strike me particularly in this way. If you came to England there would be British institutions which would strike you in this way. But let me mention three about which I feel strongly. I think, for instance, that it has been a terrible mistake in the legal system of America to put gangsters in jail for tax evasion. As soon as the law becomes a device, then the whole relation between "law of nature" and "law of man," between "is" and "ought" is lost. If you cannot jail him for keeping a string of prostitutes, you had better just let him go free. The distinction is lost as soon as the law becomes a means of manipulating people into jail because—why?—because they deserve to be in jail. What do they deserve to be in jail for? Do not ask. They deserve to be in jail. You know, that is not the scientific ethic. If you are going to put them in jail, you had better put them in jail for something fundamentally criminal.

Everybody also knows that very soon all civil services become guardians of the state as it is (this is not particularly an American phenomenon, it is a universal one). But

I do find it a very difficult situation in America that so much government money goes into scientific research, because as a result a young man who does not want to conform to what the government that day and that hour regards as proper conduct may find himself many years after in life in a very awkward state.

Finally, of course, I am very struck by the fact that once you introduce the system of the law as a device (the protection of the status quo by legal means), you finish up not with society against criminals but with two gangs: one called the police and the other called the criminals. The police wear a different kind of hat, but they have now become an army. I am, for instance, very unpleasantly struck by the fact that in my home state of California the policemen look as if they were soldiers. Policemen are not soldiers, they are guardians of the law. They are not in a campaign against crime.

Having said those things about the general tendency for the law to become an entity of its own beyond justice, what I call "the insolence of office" (I am sorry, what Shakespeare called "the insolence of office," but I am happy to steal from him), I come back to the central point about the cement of science which I now believe is the cement for any lasting community. Democracy is a way of organizing the state which has shown its success exactly as science has, because it is constantly able to transform itself. It can only do that by the same means as science, by absolute honesty and integrity. And my personal dictum about all politics is this: just make sure that everybody tells the truth all the time and tell him when he is not. You will be surprised how much notice people pay.

Certainly the intellectual's duty to complete integrity seems to me clear-cut. It seems to me clear-cut that we do not want to argue about whether these are good ends or those are good ends, whether such and such or such and such is a good form of society. We want to argue about the fact that as intellectuals we have seen the prodigious success of science as an activity because it is based on perfect trust in the truth of statements. The intellectual as a witness to truth seems to me the one thing that has to come out of this. And if I have spent five earlier lectures confusing you a great deal about just what the truth is, do not be alarmed. It is exactly because we know that we are not guardians of the truth, we do not hold any Holy Grail, that we tell the truth as best we can, and we stick to that through thick and thin.

Now having made a specific remark about American policemen, you will, I hope, allow me to end this lecture and this series of lectures with one small story just to show you that policemen are really wonderful in this country, as they are in England. In 1953 I came to M.I.T. to give the lectures on *Science and Human Values.* I had a number of misfortunes, one of which was that I was almost the first academic who came over under the new McCarran-Walter Act. I will not detail the indignities through which I was put, which ranged from being examined for venereal disease to having hastily to change my status from a professor of science to professor of history in order to get in. But finally I arrived on a cold, windy January morning on a pier in New York. And a small Irish policeman, smaller than I, faced my huge box of belongings. There had been a long list of papers which said, "What have you brought?" and so on. And I, knowing perfectly well that this was a situation in which absolute truth was much the best policy, had written down six volumes of this, and that book to give to friends, and so on. He said, "You have got all of these books?" And I said, "Yes." He said, "You know I am supposed to read all of these." I said, "Well, you know, several of the copies are identical, why don't you start?" So as bad luck would have it, he picked up a book on Blake. As I saw him handle it, I thought, "We may be in trouble, there are all kinds of references to Karl Marx, socialism and the Industrial Revolution and other taboo subjects in this." However, he read perhaps two sentences, and then he said to me, "You write this, Bud?" I said, "Yes." He said, "Psshh, this ain't never going to be no best-seller!"

So long as there are Irish policemen who are more addicted to literary criticism than to legalisms, the intellect will not perish.

INDEX

SILLIMAN VOLUMES IN PRINT

Jacob Bronowski, *The Origins of Knowledge*
S. Chandrasekhar, *Ellipsoidal Figures of Equilibrium*
Theodosius Dobzhansky, *Mankind Evolving*
René Dubos, *Man Adapting*
Ross Granville Harrison, *Organization and Development of the Embryo*
John von Neumann, *The Computer and the Brain*
Karl K. Turekian, *Late Cenozoic Glacial Ages*